Northamptonshire

Edited by Steve Twelvetree

YoungWriters
First published in Great Britain in 2004 by:
Young Writers
Remus House
Coltsfoot Drive
Peterborough
PE2 9JX
Telephone: 01733 890066
Website: www.youngwriters.co.uk

SB ISBN 1 84460 461 6

Foreword

Young Writers was established in 1991 and has been passionately devoted to the promotion of reading and writing in children and young adults ever since. The quest continues today. Young Writers remains as committed to engendering the fostering of burgeoning poetic and literary talent as ever.

This year's Young Writers competition has proven as vibrant and dynamic as ever and we are delighted to present a showcase of the best poetry from across the UK. Each poem has been carefully selected from a wealth of *Once Upon A Rhyme* entries before ultimately being published in this, our twelfth primary school poetry series.

Once again, we have been supremely impressed by the overall high quality of the entries we have received. The imagination, energy and creativity which has gone into each young writer's entry made choosing the best poems a challenging and often difficult but ultimately hugely rewarding task - the general high standard of the work submitted amply vindicating this opportunity to bring their poetry to a larger appreciative audience.

We sincerely hope you are pleased with our final selection and that you will enjoy *Once Upon A Rhyme Northamptonshire* for many years to come.

Contents

Earls Barton Junior School

Great Addington CE Primary School

Gretton Primary School

The Poems

Jess The Hamster

I have a hamster called Jess
She is always making a mess.
She plays with her toys and makes a noise when I am trying to rest.
In the morning I have to creep in case Jess is still asleep.
In her ball she rolls around, covering quite a lot of ground.
Last week I took her to the vet because she was a poorly pet,
The vet said she had an infection, so she was given an injection.
We left the vet and paid the bill and now Jess is no longer ill!

Robert Eadon (7)
Braunston CE Primary School

My Grandma

My grandma is as sweet as can be
And gives hugs and kisses to me.
My grandma's very good
And does the things the way she should.
My grandma makes
Very lovely cakes.
My grandma is a whiz
And I love her the way she is!

Constance Gough (7)
Braunston CE Primary School

Naughty Little Children

Mum, he did this, she did that,
Mum, the baby's been sick on the mat,
Mum, he's sitting on the table
Mum, she's hurting Auntie Mabel,
Naughty little children everywhere
But their mum just doesn't care.

Alicia Falcone (8)
Braunston CE Primary School

A Wyvern's Cave

Have you ever been in a wyvern's cave?
It's like getting far in a game and you forget to save.
People say they've been defeated
But they're the ones who got beaten!
Here he is now
So take your very last bow!
He fights unfair
Like a big, old grizzly bear!
With a blood-curdling scream
He's chasing you down the stream!
Now you've learnt your lesson
But the wyvern has a confession!

Marcus Banks (11)
Braunston CE Primary School

Snake

As slimy as a slug
As green as grass
As long as a rug
As fat as a glass

As spotty as a Dalmatian
As disgusting as a bug
They make quite a creation
They don't really want a hug.

Naomi Davies (8)
Braunston CE Primary School

The T-Rex

The T-rex with the twirling tail
And terrifying teeth
Terrorised the rainforest
Tracking its treat.

Luke Joel Tyson (9)
Braunston CE Primary School

The Girl

There once was a girl called Gina,
She looked very much like Sabrina,
You know that witch on TV?
Well, she isn't really, she can't be,
Anyway, back to that girl,
She had a smile like a pearl,
She looked very fine,
And was divine,
Then one day,
As old folk sadly say,
She fell off a pigsty,
Which of course, at her age, caused her to die.

Jordan Bunn (11)
Braunston CE Primary School

The River

The river is like hair rippling through slowly.
Toppling down the waterfalls with a splash.
People playing happily all day long.
So if you're down on the bank, just remember it brings peace.

Jonathan Westall (10)
Braunston CE Primary School

Haiku

Haiku, oh haiku
What a short poem you are
Five, seven, then five.

Benjamin Lord (10)
Braunston CE Primary School

The Cheetah

The cheetah is as thick as a brick.
He is not very smart.
The cheetah is as pretty as a rabbit.
His markings are a work of art.

Matthew Hurley (8)
Braunston CE Primary School

Snow - Haiku

I see snow: cold, white
Look, see soft, smooth, crispy snow.
Bright and shiny snow.

Molly-May Allinson (8)
Braunston CE Primary School

Fluffy Dog! - Haiku

Fluffy, cute, good times
I love a puppy like that!
Get one for me please!

Rhianna Sophie Crooks (8)
Braunston CE Primary School

Snow

Snow is cold like ice
It's smooth like *my* wallpaper
It's good for snow fights.

Elizabeth Hallam (8)
Braunston CE Primary School

Cats

Cats are very fluffy,
Cats are also very, very cuddly,
I love cats very much!

Jasmine Tebbutt (7)
Braunston CE Primary School

Dogs

My dog's name is Barney,
One day he was totally barmy
And knocked his brains out.

Samuel Broadley (7)
Braunston CE Primary School

Mars

Hot, dry, cold place.
Crumpled rusty surface.
Red, dark, deadly surface.

Sam Dawson (8)
Braunston CE Primary School

Dinosaurs - Haiku

They can kill their prey
Dinosaurs will stomp you down
To every last bone.

Matthew Coleman (8)
Braunston CE Primary School

Enormous Ellie

Every elephant in England eats eggs every day
But enormous Ellie gulps egg-nog every Christmas Eve
And every elephant in England gets exasperated
Because enormous Ellie gulps egg-nog every
Christmas Eve.

Tenisha Mistry (9)
Braunston CE Primary School

Happy Horse

Hannah had a happy horse called Holly
who went hunting
And they met a horse called Henry
who was at the hunt
Whose owner was called Helen.

Hannah Fitzpatrick (10)
Braunston CE Primary School

Scott The Snake

Scott the snake slithers silently
across the grass.
He is sly when he sneaks slowly
through the trees.

James Firmin (9)
Braunston CE Primary School

Cat

The creature called 'cat' is cunning and clever.
He climbs walls and he's clean
All around he calls to his companions for comfort.
He has sharp claws but when he's sleeping he's
cuddly and cute!

Amanda Jean Ford (10)
Braunston CE Primary School

Angela Anaconda

Angela Anaconda adored animals especially ants and anacondas.
She adored apples too, and ate apples every afternoon.
She gave apples to her ants and anacondas.
Her anacondas liked apples best and ate them all up.
The ants got annoyed with the anacondas because they ate
all the apples.
So the ants informed Angela and she put them in a separate
cage and all the ants and anacondas became friends.

Anika Madan (10)
Braunston CE Primary School

The Unicorn

The unicorn comes out to play.
The unicorn has a horn.
Maybe he'll come out today,
He probably goes home at dawn.

The unicorn could be a 'she',
Brushing her golden mane.
The unicorn could be a 'he',
Men are such a pain!

Harley Childs (8)
Braunston CE Primary School

Sunny Spells

Sunny spells shine steadily over Saturn
As Saturn soars around a single
Stationary sun
So when sunny spells shine steadily
Over Saturn
Saturn sucks them in so Saturn is
Scalding hot.

Helen Susan Ansell (10)
Braunston CE Primary School

Sweets

Sweets are delicious
Sweets are great
If I was allowed
I'd have them on my plate.

Some are sour
Some are sweet
Most are divine
But a few taste like feet.

But there is one
That's the best of all
It's brown and scrumptious
Chocolate, it has to rule!

Laura Cooper (11)
Braunston CE Primary School

Cars And Animals

C ars are my favourite thing,
When I hear the engine roar,
it sounds like it's going to soar
high above the hills and mountains.

A car is like a swift eagle
flying along a country road,
hoping it doesn't bump into a toad
that's on his way home for dinner.

R acing along faster than a cheetah,
blacker than a jaguar and bigger than a puma,
is it a car or a wild animal?

Jacob Tempest (10)
Braunston CE Primary School

The King's Battle

The King calls for his men to charge.
First the horses then the men at arms.
It sounds like thunder across the sky
as the cavalry charges towards the enemy's line.
The whiz of arrows, the clash of steel,
whose day will end in victory?

The King looks on, astride his sturdy steed
as his men do battle to bring the enemy to its knees.
The rain pours down as the men still fight.
The archers are gone from sight,
sword against sword is all that's left.

The King's men will not bow,
their courage and pride keep them alive.
The last of the enemy is struck and falls to ruin,
the day is victorious for King and country!

Bradley Bignell (11)
Braunston CE Primary School

Darkness

I was almost asleep,
and then darkness took me.
I was swimming in a
sea of souls dragging me
down to the darkest depths
of my heavily-built heart,
the growing anger was
winning me over and I
awoke with a shudder.

Justin Boneham (11)
Braunston CE Primary School

Roller Coaster

One. Two. Three
Zoom! We're off.
Then my brother gave a cough
I saw a flashing light. Bang!
The car in front must have had a clang
Then I saw a massive hill
My brother gave a high-pitched shrill
My heart was racing
Up and down
All the way to London town
The big hill was over
So was the ride
My brother said 'We must hide!'

Bethany Whitlow (10)
Braunston CE Primary School

War

War can be bad, war can be good,
war can cause unhappy faces,
war can cause death and despair,
war is full of banging of guns overhead,
you don't know what is happening,
you don't know what is going on,
so you hide in your little hole and pray for hope.

'Help, help!' you hear them cry.
Your fellow mates are out there dying
while you are in your hole.
That's just not right,
so you get up and fight!

Christopher Watson (10)
Braunston CE Primary School

Medieval

I wish I was a gallant knight
With a steed as white as a star
And a suit of armour shining bright
In which to ride to war.

It will be very dangerous
As we swing our maces up high
And I try to keep my shield in place
I do not want to die.

My steed could catch a nasty blow
Which would make it stumble
And I could fall with heaviness
Upon my enemy's weapon.

As they leave me here to die
I hear a faint sound of galloping hooves
I slowly raise my head to see
My faithful steed looking down at me

I grab hold of his long bloodstained mane
And I haul myself up with a great deal of pain
I pick up the reins and dig in my spurs
Making my way back to safety.

Edward Gilbert (11)
Braunston CE Primary School

My Chicken

My chicken lives on a farm,
Bigger than a barn.
He does cluck a lot but sometimes he's calm.

My chicken is a bit mad and he can be glad.
My chicken is friendly and definitely funny,
But at the moment he's sad.

Nicole Childs (8)
Braunston CE Primary School

Animals And Pets

A nimals are living things,
N ow there's some with legs and some with wings.
I n the wood you'll find squirrels and deer,
M any of them, we might fear.
A t night-time, when you go to bed,
L ots of badgers will come out instead.
S lowly and quietly hedgehogs scatter,

A s elephants stomp like it doesn't matter.
N obody cares about the snails and ants,
D o you know that they might be in your underpants?

P ets are rabbits and hamsters and cats,
E ven though my friend's got rats.
T ortoises are very rare pets,
S o they are very hard to get.

Emma Kennedy (10)
Braunston CE Primary School

The Weather

This is the weather the butterfly likes,
And so do I;
When the sun is warm and bright, floating by,
And the grass is green,
And tall and lean and children's hands are not clean,
And flowers are seen,
And children are keen,
And my friend likes the weather that's been,
And so do I!

Emily Cooksey (8)
Braunston CE Primary School

I Wish

I wish, I wish
I wish I could be
An Olympic gymnast
Like the ones on TV

They look so elegant
On floor and on vault
On bars and on beam
They make hardly a fault

They stand very proudly
With medals on chest
Knowing that they are
Simply the best.

I wish, I wish
That that could be me
An Olympic gymnast
Like the ones on TV.

Megan Lewington (10)
Braunston CE Primary School

The Monkey

Monkeys are thin and flabby,
They make me ever so cool,
They also make me happy,
But I hate it when they drool.

Monkeys swing from tree to tree,
I watch them with darting eyes,
I know it doesn't bother me,
Oops! What about when it dies?

Jemma Roughton (8)
Braunston CE Primary School

The Alien Teacher

I've never understood my teacher
Until now, you see
I've found out he's an alien
And it's as clear as can be.

He picks his nose and eats it
Likes vegetables for tea
Gives homework as a treat,
Yes my teacher is as mad as can be.

He likes watching nature shows
And singing in the bath
He thinks he's really funny,
Just because the little kids laugh.

So now I hope you realise
How mad my teacher is,
But before you start laughing, just think
He could come to your school in a whiz!

Laura Healy (11)
Braunston CE Primary School

Puzzled

I am quite puzzled.
I'm puzzled in a confusing way.
I think it's 'cause I'm having
A very puzzling day.

When people are puzzled,
They don't really want to say.
But I'd do really anything,
To get rid of my puzzling way.

Katie Bunn (10)
Braunston CE Primary School

My Planet

I went up in my spaceship
Somewhere so very far away
Travelling around in circles
I knew I couldn't find somewhere in a day.

When I finally landed on the planet
I stepped out feeling good and proud
The ground was all green and gungy
And there was no one around.

I looked in every direction
My shoes were green and sticky
Then all of a sudden I turned around
And everyone I saw looked like Mickey!

I got back in my spaceship
And flew back down to Earth
But was it all a dream
Or did I really discover Perth?

Sophie Watts (11)
Braunston CE Primary School

Thank You Nan

I have a little teddy, Jimmy he is called.
He is nearly 11 years old and his fur is going bald.
He was born in Scotland, and has tartan on his ears
but when I'm sad, he's always there to wipe away my tears.

Now I am a big girl, and like music and clothes instead
but still I keep old Jimmy Bear sat upon my bed.
So here's a great big 'Thank you!' to my Nanny Sal
for buying me 'Wee' Jimmy, my best little pal!

Kirstin Weale (10)
Braunston CE Primary School

My Baby

Tiny fingers, tiny toes,
Big blue eyes, button nose,
Smiles here, smiles there,
Smiles here and everywhere.

My baby is growing and growing,
Getting older and older,
Learning different things every day.

Cheeky face all year round,
Smiling at me every day,
This little thing, boy or girl,
Is something to treasure for life.

Even though my baby is growing up
I will always love it,
No matter what!

Katrina Edwards (11)
Braunston CE Primary School

Nutty The Squirrel

Nutty the squirrel loves to climb trees
Nutty the squirrel likes hazelnuts
Nutty the squirrel likes to eat peas
Nutty the squirrel dislikes peanuts.

Nutty the squirrel adores horse chestnuts
Nutty the squirrel likes to play dig
Nutty the squirrel likes burying nuts
When he is digging he grunts like a pig.

Robert Ansell (8)
Braunston CE Primary School

The Diver's Attic

In the diver's attic
There is a fork from the Titanic
It is bent and rusty
And half the end is missing
But it is worth more than a pot of gold.

In the diver's attic
There is a crewmember's hat from the QE2
It is covered in seaweed
And the badge rusted away
But worth as much as a Rolls Royce car.

In the diver's attic
There is a great white shark's tooth
It is covered in old rotten blood
And the end is turning black
But it is still as clean and shiny as glass.

Natalie Head (9)
Earls Barton Junior School

In The Soldier's Barracks

In the soldier's barracks
There is a rifle,
It is old, rusty and cracked
But it can shoot as fast as a jet fighter.

In the soldier's barracks,
There is a helmet,
It is thin, rusty and battered
But as hard as a rock!

Connor Aldrich (9)
Earls Barton Junior School

The Witch's Attic

In the witch's attic there is a cauldron
It is cracked, rusty and black
But as dark as the night sky.

In the witch's attic there is a spell book
It is rusty, dusty and torn
But as beautiful as new.

In the witch's attic there is a wand
It is black, white and magical
But it looks like it has just been bought.

Heather Stuart (8)
Earls Barton Junior School

An Alien Bounty Hunter's Spaceship

In the alien bounty hunter's spaceship
There is a laser gun,
It is old, cracked and dented,
But is as powerful as a plasma rifle.

In the alien bounty hunter's spaceship
There is a death stick,
It is old, dusty and bent
But it is as poisonous as a toxic dart.

Benjamin Stanbridge (9)
Earls Barton Junior School

Pirate Ship

On the pirate's ship there are some sails,
They are black, ripped and wet
But they are as big as a bed sheet.

On the pirate's ship there is a sword,
It is as old as the Earth, rusty and blunt
But as pretty as a diamond.

Oscar Francis (9)
Earls Barton Junior School

The Pirate's Cave

In the pirate's cave there is a tattered,
frayed, old map, but it still brings back
memories of ancient seas and mysteries
of treasure islands.

In the pirate's cave there is a musket
with a damaged, battered trigger,
but it fires back days when it used to
destroy its enemies.

In the pirate's cave there is a rum barrel
with a smashed and dented side but it still
holds the great smell of rum that pirates
used to drink.

In the pirate's cave there is a parrot with
a cracked and bent beak, but it remembers
and talks about when it sailed the seas.

In the pirate's cave there is a cannon
with no string to pull and fire but it still
smells of the sea when the boat used to
rock in violent waters.

Liam Bond (8)
Earls Barton Junior School

The Soldier's Barrack

In the soldier's barrack there is a gun,
It is rusty, tattered and cobwebbed
But as shiny as the moonlight in the darkness.

In the soldier's barrack there is a tin helmet,
It is dented, cracked and battered
But as hard as a Hercules.

In the soldier's barrack there is a compass,
It has a snapped hand, cracked glass and is fluffy
But is a good memory to keep.

Samuel Smith (9)
Earls Barton Junior School

The Alien's Ship

In the alien's ship there are
smashed cars but they are
still working the spirits of the
people that they have killed.

In the alien's ship there are
worn-out guns hanging on
the wall but they still echo good
times gone by.

In the alien's ship there are
rotting alien eggs but they
remind him of new life and
hopes for the future.

In the alien's ship there are
dead animals in cages but they
provide memories of their
hunting skills.

Sam Labrum (9)
Earls Barton Junior School

The Pirate's Cabin

In the pirate's cabin there is a
mouldy treasure chest but it still
holds precious gold.

In the pirate's cabin there is a
rusty cannon but it can still
shoot cannon balls.

In the pirate's cabin there is a
ripped map in ten pieces but
it still holds the secrets of
hidden treasure.

Ben Labrum (9)
Earls Barton Junior School

The Goblin's Dungeon

In the goblin's dungeon there are some bent chains,
but they are still strong enough to hold a prisoner captive.

In the goblin's dungeon there is a battered and cracked
bookshelf, but the books still hold all of the valuable secrets
of the past.

In the goblin's dungeon there is a burnt bed, but there
is still enough of it for somebody to rest on.

In the goblin's dungeon there are some smashed and
bashed potion bottles, but drops of the potion are still
inside, ready to be used.

In the goblin's dungeon there is a crumpled and torn letter
but the goblin can still see the letters of the message clearly.

In the goblin's dungeon there is a rusty gun, but it can
still protect the goblin from an enemy.

Ciara Byrne (8)
Earls Barton Junior School

The Toy Maker's Attic

In the toy maker's attic there is a train
It is rusty, old and broken
But is as good as new.

In the toy maker's attic there is a wooden doll
It is splintered, scratched and worn out
But moves like never before.

In the toy maker's attic there is a string puppet
It is broken, dusty and split
But works like a brand new puppet.

Charlotte Brown (9)
Earls Barton Junior School

The Witch's Loft

In the witch's loft, there is a
snapped broomstick but it still
flies as high as the stars.

In the witch's loft there are some
old tattered spell books but they
still hold magical spells ready
to be used.

In the witch's loft there is a
rusty cauldron but it still bubbles
like a saucepan.

In the witch's loft there is a
battered, tatty, stolen treasure
chest but it still holds wonderful
gleaming treasure.

In the witch's loft there is a holey
cloak but it still keeps her as
warm as a bear's fur.

In the witch's loft there is a dusty
old cobweb but it still sparkles
like silver in the sunlight.

In the witch's loft there are
broken floorboards but they
never ever creak.

In the witch's loft there is a
cracked window but it will never shatter.

Alexandra Smith (8)
Earls Barton Junior School

Pirate's Cabin

In the pirate's cabin there is a
corroded cannon but you can still
fire balls from it.

In the pirate's cabin there are some
rotten biscuits but they bring back
memories of the taste.

In the pirate's cabin there are some
smashed bottles but they still hold
a scent of rum.

In the pirate's cabin there is torn
and tattered maps but they still lead
to unfound treasure.

In the pirate's cabin there is a rickety
bookcase but it is still strong enough
to hold a picture of pirate secrets.

George Henry (8)
Earls Barton Junior School

In The Witch's Kitchen

In the witch's kitchen there is a wand,
It is dusty, black and old
But the magic is like a flowing river.

In the witch's kitchen there is a cat,
It is old, black and dusty
But still fast enough to catch mice.

In the witch's kitchen there is a robe,
It is old, dusty and ripped
But still able to be worn.

Hannah Tyrer (9)
Earls Barton Junior School

The Witch's Staircase

Under the witch's staircase,
there is a pile of blackened photos,
but they can tell memorable stories.

Under the witch's staircase,
there's a book of spells but it still
contains magical rhymes and phrases.

The smelly book of spells sits on an
old, tattered stool which still holds the
weight of the witch.

Under the witch's staircase, there is a
chipped mirror but it is still able to tell
how people once looked so elegant.

Under the witch's staircase, the dust
is scattered about but you can still the
the carpet's depth.

Lois Brennan (9)
Earls Barton Junior School

In The Explorer's Attic

In the explorer's attic
There is a cow's brain
It is mouldy, maggoty and gooey
But softer than a cushion.

In the explorer's attic
There is a pair of binoculars
They are rusty, tatty and broken
But shinier than the sun.

Edward Kilcoyne (9)
Earls Barton Junior School

In The Ogre's Cellar

In the ogre's cellar there is a mop,
It is smelly and has the stench of grotty soil
But it still cleans as fast as a kettle boils.

In the ogre's cellar there is an axe,
It is seven eighths of a million years old
But its silver glint still glows bold.

In the ogre's cellar, there is a skeleton,
It is scattered across the cellar, there are
Four ribs (half-eaten) hanging off the walls
And the shoulder blades are crawling with earwigs,
But it still glows like metal.

Zach Brookes (8)
Earls Barton Junior School

Magician's Attic

In the magician's attic there is a wand
It is dark, smelly and dirty
But it is as powerful as a witch's broomstick.

In the magician's attic there is a cauldron
It is powerful, murky and dirty
But it is as bubbly as a bubble bath.

In the magician's attic there is a cloak
It is ugly, ripped and bloody
But it smells like a rose.

William Carter (8)
Earls Barton Junior School

The Mermaid's Cave

In the mermaid's cave there is a
cracked gold-edged mirror . . . but it
still reflects the beautiful fish and
the sunlight which shines through
the water.

In the mermaid's cave, there is a
tattered sea dress which the
mermaid used to wear to sea
parties at the shipwreck . . . but it
still brings back memories.

In the mermaid's cave there are
lots of broken seashells . . . but they
can still be used for a beautiful,
colourful decoration.

In the mermaid's cave there is
some tangled seaweed . . . but it
can still be used as string for
party bracelets.

In the mermaid's cave there is a
snapped comb . . . but the mermaid
still can comb her long, golden
hair with it.

In the mermaid's cave there are
ripped and torn books . . . but they
are still useful to read them over
and over again.

In the mermaid's cave there are a
few chipped crystals and gems . . .
but they still twinkle in the moonlight.

In the mermaid's cave there is
soggy sand at the bottom . . . but it
can still be used as a comfy sea bed.

In the mermaid's cave there is a
damaged treasure chest . . . but it
still holds beautiful jewels and gold.

In the mermaid's cave there are
dented rocks . . . but they can still be
used to sit on.

Yasmin Moussa (8)
Earls Barton Junior School

In The Dragon's Cave

In the dragon's cave,
There is some gold,
It is ancient, hard and yellow,
But reflects the light,
Like lights in the darkest place on Earth

In the dragon's cave there are some eggs,
They are black, large and cracked,
But they are warm within,
And will bring happiness to the cave.

Anthony Kenny (9)
Earls Barton Junior School

The Pirate's Cabin

In the pirate's cabin there is a parrot
with a broken wing but you can still
see its beautiful colours.

In the pirate's cabin there is a gun
with no shots left but it still holds
memories of pirate hands.

In the pirate's cabin there is a jail
with a dented, bent door but it can
still be locked and hold men within it.

Sam Whittet (9)
Earls Barton Junior School

In The Mermaid's Kingdom

In the mermaid's kingdom there is a boot,
It is battered, stained and ancient,
But it still brings back wonderful memories.

In the mermaid's kingdom there is a human statue,
It is tarnished, old and dusty,
But glimmers in the sunlight, like a glittery star
In the frosty sky.

In the mermaid's kingdom there is a sword,
It is tatty, soiled and antiquated,
But it shines like a moonlit night sky.

In the mermaid's kingdom there is a chest,
It is rotten, dirty and smelly,
But it still keeps money as safe as the Queen's bank.

Sophie Child (8)
Earls Barton Junior School

The Wizard's Wardrobe

In the wizard's wardrobe you will find
splintered glass from the potion
that still holds secrets of his powers!

In the wizard's wardrobe there are
aged, dark, dusty cobwebs but they
are still home to the tarantulas,
their hairy legs quivering towards their prey.

In the wizard's wardrobe there is a
crumpled picture of the wizard's father
but the pieces still fit together.

Sam Saunders (8)
Earls Barton Junior School

The Witch's Cellar

In the witch's cellar there is a broomstick
It is splintered, twisted and crooked
But it still whizzes through the air like a rocket
Zooming through space.

In the witch's cellar there is a wand
It is snapped, filthy and bent
But the magic still sparkles out like the sparks
Whizzing out of a sparkler.

In the witch's cellar there is a spell book
It is dusty, ripped and creased
But the golden pages still shine like the crown
On the Queen's head.

Connor Wisdom (9)
Earls Barton Junior School

In The Captain's Cabin

In the captain's cabin there is a medallion,
it is black, rusty and scratched
but still makes the curse for the pirates
who have the black pearl.

In the captain's cabin there is a map,
it is torn, ripped and old
but still lights the way to the treasure.

In the captain's cabin there is a sword,
it is rusty, tarnished and bent
but at the end it is as shiny as a shooting star
whizzing through the night sky.

Jonathon Clewer (8)
Earls Barton Junior School

The Explorer's Shipwreck

In the explorer's shipwreck there is a leopard-skin rug.
It is battered, torn and burnt
But in the wind it still roars like it still lives.

In the explorer's shipwreck there is a human skeleton
It is chipped and mossy
But at night its spirit searches for a body to live in again.

In the explorer's shipwreck there is a Zulu warrior's spear and shield
They are chipped, cracked and burnt
But still can fight another 100 wars.

In the explorer's shipwreck there is an Air Force One statue.
It is worn out, battered and chipped
But when nobody looks it flies out of the shipwreck
Like a twinkling star shining on a frosty winter's night.

In the explorer's shipwreck there are a dozen books about animals
They are battered and torn, ripped pages are missing
And so are some photos
But they still give more information than the Grand Library.

Abbie Tipler (9)
Earls Barton Junior School

The Old Cook's Kitchen

In the old cook's kitchen there is a wooden spoon
It is brown, stained and smelly
But it's a good antique.

In the old cook's kitchen there is an old cooker
It is dented, cracked and disgusting
But as powerful as a tornado.

In the old cook's kitchen there is some old cutlery
It is rusty, bent and not very steady
But tiny powerful bits of silver still show.

Hannah Lee (8)
Earls Barton Junior School

The Scientist's Attic

In the scientist's attic, there is a piece of crystal,
It is rotten, rusty and battered.
But it is still ablaze when the sunlight hits it.

In the scientist's attic there is a dinosaur's bone,
It is old, boring and dull.
But it still brings back old memories of what it must have been like.

In the scientist's attic there is a piece of turtle shell,
It is faint, filthy and grubby,
But it still hides you like a shadow of an old tree.

In the scientist's attic there is an old elephant's tusk,
It is old, tattered and brown,
But it is still as sharp as a steak knife.

Chelsie Freeman (9)
Earls Barton Junior School

In The Fairy's House

In the fairy's house there is a wand
It is crooked, dirty and dusty
But it still sparkles like a twinkling star.

In the fairy's house there is an old pot
It is smashed and black with soot
But it still holds fairy dust and glitters
Like a golden treasure chest.

In the fairy's house there is a mirror
It is smashed and battered
But it still shines like a shimmering star.

Maisie Garthwaite (8)
Earls Barton Junior School

The Spy's Den

In the spy's den there is a spy gun climber.
It is tarnished, jammed and rusty,
But a bit is not tarnished and glows in the sun like a ruby.

In the spy's den there is a glow in the dark glasses.
They are smashed and bent,
But they still shine in the dark like a torch.

In the spy's den there is a water gun.
It is scratched and sometimes blocked,
Bu it still squirts water like a whale.

In a spy's den there are X-ray glasses
They are broken and the armour is snapped,
But they still look through things like an X-ray.

Alix Daverson (8)
Earls Barton Junior School

The Eskimo's Igloo

In the Eskimo's igloo there is a fishing rod -
It is bent, crooked and smelly,
But still as strong as an elephant.

In the Eskimo's igloo there is a fur coat -
It is ripped, tattered and the zip is broken,
But still as cosy as the warmest bed.

In the Eskimo's igloo there is a pile of cups
And plates made of ice -
They are chipped, cracked and dusty,
But still glitter like the stars at night.

Rachel Bedster (8)
Earls Barton Junior School

In The Demon's Den

In the demon's den there are some chains
They are bloody, rusty and tarnished
But they still glint like a star in the frosty air.

In the demon's den there is a knife,
It is rough, dusty and ancient
But it still cuts through wood like a big axe chopping down a tree.

In the demon's den there is a cauldron,
It is old, cracked and smelly,
But it still shines like lots of gold in the sun.

In the demon's cave there are some masks,
They are ripped, tatty and split,
But they still fit round your head like the Earth going round the sun.

Samantha Atherley (9)
Earls Barton Junior School

The Blacksmith's Shop

In the blacksmith's shop there is a sword,
It is mucky, bloodstained and sharp
But as silvery as Excalibur.

In the blacksmith's shop there are arrowheads,
They're blunt, hard and rusty
But as valuable as gold.

In the blacksmith's shop there are horseshoes,
They are old, rusty and dented
But they shimmer like the sun.

William Leabon (8)
Earls Barton Junior School

In The Witch's Kitchen

In the witch's kitchen there is a wand,
It is battered, bent and splintered
But it still has magic running through it like a man
on a running track.

In the witch's kitchen there is a cloak and hat
They are ripped, ragged and frayed
But they are still as dark as a stormy night sky.

In the witch's kitchen there are potion pots
They are smashed at the top, stained and cracked
But they still hold potions like a volcano holding lava.

In the witch's kitchen there is a spell book
It is torn, has pages missing and dusty
But it is still as powerful as Merlin's powers put together.

In the witch's kitchen there is a cauldron
It is tarnished, smelly and melted
But it still holds potions and mixes them like the wind.

Florence Blackadder (8)
Earls Barton Junior School

Magician's Attic

In the magician's attic there is a cloak,
It is black, bloody and has dead animal fur,
But it is as soft as a cushion.

In the magician's attic there is a clock,
It is cracked, rusty and dirty,
But it is as red as a rose.

In the magician's attic there is a hat,
It is black, dusty and ripped,
But it is as smooth as a glass cup.

Lauren Reece (9)
Earls Barton Junior School

In The Mum's Kitchen

In the mum's kitchen there is a mop,
It is twisted, torn and cracked,
But it can still let the mum mop the floor so it shines like the sun.

In the mum's kitchen there is a cooker,
It is wobbly, rusty and dirty,
But it can still make the dinner as fresh as the sea.

In the mum's kitchen there is a fridge,
It is battered, splintered and chipped,
But it is still as heavy as gold.

In the mum's kitchen there is a shelf,
It is tea-stained, worn out and weak,
But it can still wobble like the Queen's crown.

In the mum's kitchen there is a pair of glasses,
They are half-demolished, cracked and damaged,
But the other half of the glasses shines like the sun shines
off the sea.

Ben Nolan (9)
Earls Barton Junior School

The Builder's Attic

In the builder's attic there is a pair of goggles.
Old, cracked and rusty
But as shiny as gold.

In the builder's attic there is a cement mixer,
Dusty, and squeaky
But as pretty as a princess.

In the builder's attic there is a pair of overalls,
They are dirty and torn
But as good as new.

Robyn Henderson (9)
Earls Barton Junior School

In The Queen's Parlour

In the Queen's parlour there is a mirror,
It is smashed, tarnished and dusty,
But it still shows reflections like the symmetry on a butterfly.

In the Queen's parlour there is a picture,
It is cracked, battered and broken,
But it brings back memories of when she was a child.

In the Queen's parlour there is a bin,
It is piled high, stuffed and overflowing with paper,
But it reminds her of her grandfather who gave it to her.

In the Queen's parlour there is a crown,
It is dented, ripped and filthy
But it reminds her she is Queen.

In the Queen's parlour there is a gown,
It is torn, faded and frayed,
But it is as beautiful as a sunny day in winter.

Heather Collis (9)
Earls Barton Junior School

The Magician's Attic

In the magician's attic there is a clock,
It is cracked, smashed and goes the wrong way,
But it shines like the sun and it looks new.

In the magician's attic there is a broomstick,
It is bashed and broken and has been run into a tree,
But is as black as a pitch-black sky.

In the magician's attic there is a wand,
It is rusty and when you cast a spell it does it back to you,
But it is as black as the darkest sky.

Jay Smith (9)
Earls Barton Junior School

In The Former Warrior's Attic

In the former warrior's attic there is armour
It is battered, the warrior's symbol has fallen off and is cracked
But it still glints in the sunlight like a mirror.

In the former warrior's attic there is a shield
It is chipped, burned and the strap has come off
But you could not get hit behind it.

In the former warrior's attic there is a sword
It is rusty, the hand protector has fallen off and it is dusty
But it will still fight like a wrestler.

In the former warrior's attic there is a gun
It has no powder, the trigger has fallen off and it is cracked
But the metal still glints in the sunlight.

In the former warrior's attic there is a helmet
The nosepiece is gone and there are holes in it and it is tarnished
But it can still withstand a lot of force.

Jacob Humphries (9)
Earls Barton Junior School

The Cook's Kitchen

In the cook's kitchen there is a radiator,
It is broken, old and leaking
But it is as warm as a hot cup of tea.

In the cook's kitchen, there is a cooker,
It is rusty, old and broken
But the food is absolutely gorgeous.

In the cook's kitchen there are some potions,
They are cracked, steaming and poisonous
But they glow like the rainbow.

Daisy Habicher (9)
Earls Barton Junior School

In The Witch's Cellar

In the witch's cellar there is a wand.
It is old, rusty and snapped but it still
sparkles like a bright, shining moon.

In the witch's cellar there is a broomstick.
It is old, broken and snapped but it still
flies at the speed of light.

In the witch's cellar there is a cauldron.
It is rusty, tarnished and tatty but it still
burns up children.

In the witch's cellar there is a spell book.
It is tatty, scratched and old but it still
has wicked, nasty spells.

Aiden McAvoy (8)
Earls Barton Junior School

Alien's Attic

In the alien's attic there is a spacecraft,
It is black, crushed and battered
But it shines like the sun.

In the alien's attic there is a space gun,
It is black, worn-out and slimy,
But it is as deadly as a dinosaur.

In the alien's attic there is a piece of armour,
It is deserted, cracked and bent
But it is as shiny as the sun on a summer's day.

Leigh Prickett (8)
Earls Barton Junior School

In The Vampire's Dungeon

In the vampire's dungeon there is a wand,
It is elderly, chipped and cracked,
But the magic still bursts out like a firework in a hazy night.

In the vampire's dungeon there is a coffin,
It is dusty, rotten and ruined,
But the lock still shines like a golden phoenix flying over
the orange sunset.

In the vampire's dungeon there are some fangs,
They are mouldy, yellow and disintegrating,
But they still glisten in the moonlight like a silver star.

In the vampire's dungeon there is a cape,
It is cobwebby, ripped and ancient,
But the blackness is still as powerful as the night.

In the vampire's dungeon there is a pot of blood,
It is mildewed, stale and musty,
But the redness still gleams like a bonfire on a wintry night.

Laura White (9)
Earls Barton Junior School

In The Devil's Den

In the red devil's den there is a fork,
It is snapped, splintered and the flames have died off,
But the heat is still there and it still spits sparks like fireworks
zooming over the burning fire.

In the red devil's den there are bones,
They are fractured and splintered and cracked,
But they are still alive.

Jack McGrath (8)
Earls Barton Junior School

In The Teacher's Attic

In the teacher's attic there is a cane,
It is splintered, twisted and dusty.
But it still whizzes through the air
Like a page turning over from the wind.

In the teacher's attic there is a book,
It is scratched, tattered and antiquated.
But the golden pages still shine in the sunlight.

In the teacher's attic there is a bag of sweets,
They are stale, out-of-date and sour.
But the sweets still look as shiny as a twinkling
Star in the dark sky.

In the teacher's attic there is a cloak,
It is moth-eaten, torn and full of cobwebs.
But the cloak is still as black as the black sky.

In the teacher's attic there is a mortarboard,
It has lost its colour, it is as crusty as bread.
But the mortarboard is still as comfortable
As my favourite pair of shoes.

Dominique Frinke (8)
Earls Barton Junior School

The Dragon's Cave

In the dragon's cave there is a dragon
It is ugly, scary and toothless
But it is as shiny as the sun.

In the dragon's cave there are some broken dragon wings
They are holey, full of stitches and covered in maggots
But are as spotty as a Dalmatian.

Kieron Lee (8)
Earls Barton Junior School

The Magician's Mansion

In the magician's mansion there is
a demagnetised compass but it
still shows the way to magic rings.

In the magician's mansion there is
a tattered and crumpled map but it
still shows the way to lost treasure.

In the magician's mansion there is
a cut-in-half wardrobe but it still
holds his clothes.

In the magician's mansion there is
a bent and chipped sword but it
can still chop things.

In the magician's mansion there are
burnt spell books but the spells
are still clear.

In the magician's mansion there are
battered wands but they still sparkle.

In the magician's mansion there is
a melted and singed goblet but
you can still drink from it.

In the magician's mansion there is
a shrunken and misshapen cloak
but it still holds memories of the times
he wore it.

Ryan Smart (9)
Earls Barton Junior School

Pirate's Cave

In the pirate's cave, there is a
ripped-up island map, but the map
reminds him of the great adventures
of the mystery islands he has been to.

In the pirate's cave, there is a
dented sword but the sword reminds
him of the great battles he has fought.

In the pirate's cave there is a
broken treasure chest with dirty treasure
inside but it echoes the memories of
great treasure-hunting days.

In the pirate's cave there is a
rusty anchor but the anchor reflects
the life-saving days of long-lost islands.

In the pirate's cave there is a
dusty cannon but the cannon can still
shoot cannonballs and destroy other ships.

In the pirate's cave there is a
squeaky parrot, but if you place him
close against your ear, you can still
hear him talk.

In the pirate's cave, there is a
torn jacket, but it can still be worn by
pirates for sailing the seven seas.

In the pirate's cave, there is a
splintered plank, but pirates can still
use it to walk intruders to their death.

In the pirate's cave, there are
tailless rats, but the rats can still
creep up on people unexpectedly.

Daniel Turner (9)
Earls Barton Junior School

The Diver's Wardrobe

In the diver's wardrobe there is a torch
It is dull, blue and the batteries are worn down
But is as powerful as the sun.

In the diver's wardrobe there is an anchor
It is rusty, black and cracked
But could hold down the Titanic.

In the diver's wardrobe there is an air tank
It is still, cold and cracked
But is like fresh air.

Matthew Whatton (9)
Earls Barton Junior School

In A Boy's Bedroom

In the boy's bedroom there is a Yu-Gi-Oh card
It is ripped, curled and tatty.
But it is the best card in the world.

In the boy's bedroom there is a chair
It is frayed, battered and torn.
But it is as comfortable as a bed.

In the boy's bedroom there is a shelf
It is splintered, chipped and battered.
But still holds trophies like a man.

Antonio Graziano (9)
Earls Barton Junior School

In The Dragon's Cave

In the dragon's cave there is a dragon's scale
It is scratched, menacing and grimy
But it is still as sharp as a shark's tooth
And gleams like a sun close up.

In the dragon's cave there is a ball of fire
It is flickering, antique and boiling
But it is still as hot as fire.

In the dragon's cave there is a skeleton
It is trashed, crunched and smashed
But it is as white as a snowy day and steams like an oven.

Robert McArdle (8)
Earls Barton Junior School

How To Become A Clown

Preparation time: 3 hours

Ingredients: red nose, gigantic boots, curlers/permers
big dungarees, wobbly knees.

Method:
Wear a red nose that goes *toot!*
Buy some gigantic boots,
Buy some curlers,
Or some permers,
Then make your hair go *katoot!*

Buy some big dungarees,
You need some wobbly knees,
You need to be exciting,
We want no biting,
And do funny things like climb up trees.

Faye Murray (10)
Exeter Junior School

How To Become A Clown

Preparation time: 1 hour.

Ingredients: Face painting
Spiky wig.
One-wheel bike.

Method:
There once was a man called Charlie Frown,
Who wanted to become a clown,
He had to learn lots of silly stunt training,
And juggle steak knives through the town.
'The circus is big just like your wig,
I'm sure you will be good for a gig.
Making kids laugh, you'll talk to the giraffe,
OK, Frown, you are a fully-paid clown.'

Lyndsay-Ann Carson (11)
Exeter Junior School

How To Become . . . A Clown

Preparation time: 1 hour

Ingredients: face paint, big shoes, chair, clothes, balloons.

Method:
There once was an old man who lived in a town,
He wanted so much to become a clown,
With his fuzzy-wuzzy hair,
He'd sit in his chair,
With a wonky-donky sad frown.

With his big, clumpy shoes, he'd slap and snooze,
His white face splashed in ooze,
Making people laugh he'd sit in the bath,
With colourful baggy old clothes
Giving children red and yellow balloons.

Nikki Hughes (11)
Exeter Junior School

How To Become A Clown

Preparation time: five minutes

Ingredients: red nose, town, red rose, gold crown, shiny bowl

Method:
There was an old man who wanted to be a clown,
And so put on his golden crown,
Next on went his red nose,
And he tied on his red rose,
Then ran all the way to town.

He put on his shiny bow,
So it would make a good show.
He sat on the floor,
And said, 'I can do much more'
Finally told the children to sit in a row.

Lianne Bright (10)
Exeter Junior School

How To Become A Clown

Preparation time: It will take two hours to become a clown.

Ingredients: Face paint, red nose, big shoes, baggy clothes, fussy hair.

Method:
There once was a man called Scott,
His wife thought he'd lost the plot,
When he juggled all night,
Wore hair oh, so bright,
And laughed himself into a knot.
'I know what I'm doing, my dear,
From this I will make my career,
Sew on my trousers a patch,
Make my shoes big to match,
And for my sanity, please have no fear!'

Sam Dale (10)
Exeter Junior School

How To Become . . . A Clown

Preparation time: Two hours

Ingredients: Make-up, hat, bow, cash, boat, penny.

Method:
A child cried and cried,
Then a man appeared from outside.
He told him a joke
Then he began and spoke,
'You're a funny old sir,' he said,
'You can become a clown you know.
All you need is a hat and a bow.
Then you'll be off in a flash,
To spend all your cash,
And then stomp on a classical boat,
You'll be off and away,
And the kids will all stay
To watch you again and again.

You'll have a good laugh, what more can I say?
Then we'll all go and play.
You'll be chanting some funny rhymes,
All of the time,
And you'll never be bored again.
I'll have good luck, don't you see?
You will be a very special clown as good as can be.
Plus, you mean a lot to me.'

Sarah L Small (10)
Exeter Junior School

View From My Window

Sitting by the window watching the robin bobbing along.
Cars going *screech,* as they speed down the street.
Looking at a kite flying to the light.
Looking at that cat staring at that rat.
Looking at the car in the car park.
Going into McDonald's, having a 'McFlurry'.

James Cox (9)
Exeter Junior School

How To Become A Clown

Preparation time: six hours.

Ingredients: van, circus, dog, knives, town.

Method:
There was a young man called Jamie Brown.
Who wanted to become a clown.
His nickname was Dan
He arrived in a van
Because he heard of a circus in town.

He went to the circus to get a job
They said, 'You must juggle a dog!
You must also do stunts,
Like juggling knives that are blunt!
Off you go and change into a frog!'

Zoe O'Rourke (10)
Exeter Junior School

View From My Window

I rise from my bed and look out of my window.
Some cars, lorries, tanks, leak.
I feel gentle breezes.
Birds swooping past.
I smell McDonald's burgers
And I can taste the cars' fumes.

I see lots of people walking past.
The ground tremors with construction sites.
Now I close my window and curtains
And I walk away.

Thomas Lamont (10)
Exeter Junior School

How To Become A Clown

Preparation time: 59 mins 59 sec

Ingredients: green hair, purple bees, roses, bleeping red nose, humongous shoes

Method:
To give him green hair eat milky cheese,
Put swirls in your ears and eat purple bees,
To buy baggy clothes put a rose in your nose,
To learn to do stunts chomp a red nose
And make sure you have knobbly knees.

Wear a bleeping red nose,
Wear large funny clothes,
Put on your humongous shoes,
Which must be green and blue,
Paint your fingers and toes,
Then you'll look like a rose,
And that is how to become a clown.

Danielle Wilson (11)
Exeter Junior School

The Moon

The full moon is like a silver ball spinning peacefully,
like a giant eye gazing at you,
like a gigantic gobstopper whizzing around your hair,
like a giant mirror sitting there swallowing.

The changing moon is like a mouth opening and closing,
nibbling through cheese like a hammock swaying,
like a segment orange just sitting waiting for you,
like a bite of a biscuit being eaten slowly.

Megan Cowan (8)
Exeter Junior School

How To Become A Clown

Preparation time: 1 hour

Ingredients: Red bow, paste.

Method:
There once was a man called Crown,
He wanted to become a clown.
He wore a red bow,
So it would show,
With his white face
All covered in paste.

To make the children laugh
I just walk down the path,
I just make them laugh,
By tripping up the staff.

Katie Morgan (10)
Exeter Junior School

The Moon

The changing moon is like a yellow banana
sitting quietly in the bowl.
Like a wet hammock swinging in the rain.
Like an old fishing boat with old cracks
on the floor of it.
Like a dark brown hair clip sitting in wet hair.

The full moon is like a white egg standing in the cold
freezing like a model.
Like a bouncy ball bouncing on the bumpy path.
Like a grey, round stone rolling down the sharp,
rocky mountain.
Like a white eye staring at you in the café.

Kieran Gourley (9)
Exeter Junior School

How To Become A Clown

Preparation time: till late

Ingredients: purple crown, red balloon, baggy purple trousers,
Gigantic boots, black leather belt, circus, laughs.

Method:
Today a man called Plown
Wanted to become a clown,
He came with a man,
In a colourful van
And head of a circus in town.

So he bought a purple crown,
In this extraordinary town
And walked along the path,
Trying to laugh,
This man is now a very funny clown.

Claudio Moreira (11)
Exeter Junior School

How To Become A Clown

Preparation time: two minutes
Ingredients: face paints, red nose, frizzy izzy hair and funny clothes.

Method:
Two minutes ago a man kicked his toe,
He is a clown but he wore a frown,
So he jumped up and down and juggled gold crowns,
But now he is so very slow.

A man walked by but looked so shy.
The clown looked and started to cry,
He fell on his knees and got stung by a bee
So he said, 'You can't just walk by and look shy!'

Nicola James (11)
Exeter Junior School

How To Become A Clown

Preparation time: hall night

Ingredients: baggy colourful trousers, bright red nose, gigantic boots, squeezy flower, pink crown, laughter, full circus, green soft jumper, face painters (make-up).

Method:
There was once a brown clown,
Who was juggling large hoops in my town,
He once came with a man,
The man had a red coke can,
He was once a funny clown.

His real name is Pown,
Now he ain't down,
The man's name is Bob,
He gave him a job,
The clown received a pink clown.

Ruijorge Branco Da Silva (10)
Exeter Junior School

Through My Window

As I look out my window I glance at the trees
it looks rather bare because it has no leaves

As I open my window I lean on the sill
and I see the postman delivering a nasty bill

When my window is open I smell the fresh air
it goes up my nose and blows my hair

When I wake up in the morning I hear the blackbirds
they chirp so loudly it gets on my nerves

As I open my window I taste bacon and egg
I wonder who's cooking, maybe it is Meg.

Daniel McSkimming (10)
Exeter Junior School

How To Be A Good Aunty

How to be a good aunty,
Take them different places,
Make them feel happy,
Make sure they take good paces.

Have a laugh,
Swap some love,
Help them have a bath,
Love them even more.

Play with them,
Draw as well,
Help them to learn
And take them to school.

Louise Sheehan (11)
Exeter Junior School

Through The Window

When I spot a steep hill,
It is always the size of a windmill.

If my hands feel a little cat,
It's wearing a large brown hat.

When I listen to zooming cars,
They're driving across the old road tar.

As I sampled some yummy chips,
I saw a man with a box at his hips.

As I sniff unleaded gas,
It even comes through the window glass.

Myles Sadler (9)
Exeter Junior School

The Moon

The full moon is like a shiny marble
Like a headlight staring into space
Like a round plate drifting through plants
Like a wheel silently staring at the moon
Like a shiny eye staring at Earth
Like a massive disco ball spinning around the Earth
Like a button moving around the Earth.

The changing moon is like a happy mouth
Beaming over the land
Like a Viking longboat sailing across an island
Like a boomerang flying across the moon
Like a stone stuck on the moon's surface.

Stefan Earle (9)
Exeter Junior School

Through The Window

As I watch a brown cat,
perched on the sill it sat.

I could scent some toxic gas,
while still staring at the grass.

I could prefer some yummy fries,
and see a dog with googly eyes.

I could discover a rusty van,
driven by an old man.

I could stroke a shiny car,
driving in the sticky tar.

George Allan (9)
Exeter Junior School

How To Be A Good Sister

If you want to be a good sister
Just listen to what they say
Always take them out with you
Never send them away.

Give them as much love as they need
Never leave them out
Never lose your temper
Never have a doubt.

So listen to me now
Always hold them tight
Give them a cuddle every day
Never let them out of sight.

Leanne Noonan (11)
Exeter Junior School

Recipe For A Mythical Creature

Add a white tail as long as a grey trunk.
Peel soft white feet as short as cats' paws.
Fry thin legs the size of a ruler.
Drain a big mouth as loud as an elephant.
Stir white skin as soft as snow.
Mix some eyes like the blue sea.
Stir a black, slimy nose like the night sky.
Boil some floppy ears like dead flowers.
Chop a wide body like a big door.
Dry a soft white head as soft as a fluffy teddy.
Refresh a pointy chin like a sharp nail.

Nicola Pringle (8)
Exeter Junior School

Recipe For A Mythical Creature

Add a tail as long as a tree trunk.
A head as pointed as the edge of a cliff.
Like slashed feather.
Eyes as red as blood.
Fry well until you hear a swooshing noise.
Boil the teeth to make them warm.
Chop its legs into little tiny pieces.
Slice strips off the back.
Let the head dry then cool it for 20 minutes.

Beth Martin (8)
Exeter Junior School

Mythical Creature

Add a head as shadowy as leather
and some eyes as piercing as bulletpoints.
Slice some red rose skin
and stir with a drip of magic.
Then fry breath of fresh cut flowers
then keep in a dark forest for six days
and serve on the side of the moon.

Ben Finan (9)
Exeter Junior School

How To Be A Good Sister

To be a good sister you need to laugh.
To be a good sister you need to give half.
To be a good sister you need to share.
To be a good sister you need to care.

Some people say a sister's your best friend
But sometimes they send you round the bend!

Stefanie Thomson (11)
Exeter Junior School

View From My Window

Here I sit by my window sill,
Looking at Mother Nature's glamorous garden,
I smell the fragrant plants and I hear the joyful songs of birds,
The gigantic trees are home to animals, so is the soft, damp soil.

Lovely lakes with a satisfying swaying back and forth,
The water is so clear it looks so transparent,
You can always see little fishes swimming to the waterfall and back.

If you go outside, you feel the air swiftly floating between your fingers,
You hear birds flapping, I see foxes sleeping in burrows
And the sun shining, making the plants grow.

You can taste the jasmine in the non-polluted air,
But now I don't want to look out of my window, because
People have built over this land.

All it is now is a polluted wasteland,
Cars are screeching and smashing,
Graffiti on walls, restaurants and more houses.

I can never get to sleep at night,
God, where have you put the light?

Kai Smales (10)
Exeter Junior School

Through The Window

I spy a fluffy cat
Resting on the sill it sat.
The feel of cracks
Go in very short tracks.
The smell of stinky fumes
So, so high it looms.
The sound of a little mouse
Squeaking in the old house.
The taste of luscious fries
'Don't eat me,' it cries.

Ryan Baines (9)
Exeter Junior School

View From The Window

Early in the morning
Before the sun went up
The car's engines banging
Nearly woke me up.

Outside my window
There's houses all around
There's shops, markets and even McDonald's
There's buildings all around.

Outside my window
There's a lot of cars around
Zooming past my garden
It is always so loud.

Just before I go to bed
I watch outside my window
All I can see is lights
And I glance all night.

Liam Difolco (10)
Exeter Junior School

Mythical Creature

Add a long body as wide as a table and a fiery tail.
A fin as sharp as a shark's top.
A tummy as fat as a giant's.
Mix skin like slimy alligator scales.
Wings as big as two houses shaped like a V.
Weapons as red as a big fire ball.
His breath is as fiery as fire.
Teeth as sharp as a knife.
Claws as sharp as a fork.
Two horns like a witch's hat.
Toes shaped like furry caterpillars.
Eyes as angry as a rhino charging.

Ryan Davies (8)
Exeter Junior School

View From My Window

In the early hours of the day,
I saw a beautiful bird.

In the early hours of the day,
I heard someone talking.

In the early hours of the day,
I spied on a cat.

In the early hours of the day,
I smelt a pizza.

In the early hours of the day,
I felt a car vibrating.

In the early hours of the day,
I tasted petrol.

Craig Mahon (9)
Exeter Junior School

View From My Window

I can smell burgers with cheese.
I would really, really like one please.

I can see a little shop,
In and out people pop.

I can hear children chatting,
And the big dog with them they are patting.

Do I dare touch the car,
Parked in the sticky tar?

I can taste chips,
I greedily lick my lips.

Ayrton Aitchison (9)
Exeter Junior School

View From The Window

In the early hours of morning
It was never so boring.

The birds sing in the sky,
Parrots over my house fly.

I look out the window and see cats
Running around chasing a rat.

But now those days are gone
And I feel like I am alone.

I can't see the birds in the sky
Or the parrots fly.

There are no cats chasing rats
Only silver zooming cars.

And dirty smelly chocolate bars.

Nebojsa Augustinov (10)
Exeter Junior School

The Moon

The full moon is like a bouncing ball.
Like a white eye staring into space.
Like a white button on a black coat.

The crescent moon is like a banana sitting in a black fruit bowl.
Like a tiger's claw scratching the air.
Like a rowing boat sailing the seven seas.
Like a boomerang flying around the multicoloured earth.

Matthew Cleary (8)
Exeter Junior School

The View From The Window

I spy a shop
with a sign on top.

I can smell some fries
when I talk to guys.

I can hear a car on the road
and a lorry with a heavy load.

I can smell everyone's food
when I look at the world.

I can see someone touching a tree
and my friend Lee.

Darryl Cluff (9)
Exeter Junior School

View From My Window

Early in the morning,
The birds awaken me.

Cats softly miaowing,
Dogs loudly barking.

Babies screaming like mad,
Bees buzzing round and round.

Leaves rustling and blowing,
Colourful graffiti on the wall.

Delicious smelling pizza,
McDonald's yummy smell.

Hollie Spowart (10)
Exeter Junior School

View From My Window

In the early hours of dawn
The roaring of car engines wake me up.

The screeching of brakes startles me.

I see the smoke of factories
I have to stop this pollution,
It's destroying our world.

I see children laughing joyfully
One day they will realise what's
Happening to our world.

Roaring machines and the screeching of brakes
Make me appreciate Mother Nature,
Life for the homeless is dreadful,
I appreciate what I have
Is there no solution to stop this pollution?

Paula-J Scott (10)
Exeter Junior School

Mythical Creature

Add a head as huge as a tree.
Cut the shape like a balloon.
A body as fat as a trunk.
It can fly as fast as a rocket.
Body as tall as a pyramid.
Add wings that shimmer and glisten.
It runs as fast as a cheetah.
The skin is like metal.
Add a tail as long as Mount Everest.
Blend some cars that shine
And arms that are short as mouse legs.

Bradley Everett (8)
Exeter Junior School

View From My Window

I hear the shouting babies
Standing next to the ladies.

I smell the perfumed flowers,
Making me have powers.

I taste the appetising food,
Making me in a good mood.

I see the people chat
Calling me a brat.

I feel the cold air
Going through my hair.

I hear the roaring traffic,
Even when I am in my attic.

The howling dogs and the yelling cats,
The forest is much better than that,
But Mother Nature can never come back
But I hope and dream it will.

Emma Joseph (10)
Exeter Junior School

How To Be A Good Footballer

If you want to be a footballer
you need to eat healthy food and keep fit.

You can work hard and train
but when you pass you need to use your brain.

Be positive and take someone on and you might score.
If you do score a goal, your wage rises even higher.

Then you will definitely be a millionaire.
You need to practise your skills
like shooting, passing, control, tricks and goal scoring.

Adam Witt (11)
Exeter Junior School

View From My Window

In the early hours of twilight,
I love the wind blowing against the trees
Swaying side to side,
The birds flying away, migrating to the south,
Thinking to myself, *will I see it again? Will I see it again?*
Cats miaowing continuously,
Long slender blades of grass,
Aged trees' bark peeling off,
The jasmine's smell reminds me of my
Next-door neighbour's cats purring for food,
But now it's all changed,
There's roaring cars and the revving motorbikes,
Wrappers and rubbish lying on the street,
Now there's rows and rows of houses,
No more hills, no more trees.

Paige Redden (10)
Exeter Junior School

View Through The Window

As I watch the light blue sky,
I notice it is very high.

When I stroke the friendly cat,
Upon the wooden fence it sat.

Upon my lips I feel some yummy chips,
Then I see someone swaying their bony hips.

Then I pick up a speedy cat,
Driving on the black tar.

I smell the scent of sugary tea,
It is very yummy for me.

Emily Wyles (10)
Exeter Junior School

When I Looked Through My Window

I spy a shop,
With a dirty top.

As I touched a cat,
I realised it was fat.

I like the smell of chips
And I lick my lips.

I hear a kite,
With a high flight.

I tasted some chips,
And I saw some pips.

Lauren Angieri (9)
Exeter Junior School

Through The Window

As I perceive a metal shed
I was eating a loaf of bread.

When I smell the diesel garage
Cam's car slowed down like a horse and carriage.

I love petting my furry cat
Lying on the window sill mat.

As I hear the tinkling car
Driving on the bumpy tar.

When I taste the salty fries
Just a hint I taste a pie!

Daisy Finan (9)
Exeter Junior School

Mythical Creature

Add
Eyes as red as fire,
Skin as yellow as flowers,
Legs as blue as the sky.

Mix
A body as fat as a giant,
Wings as brown as beans,
Ears as thin as a wire.

Decorate
Feet as soft as blond hair,
Tail as thin as a nose
Teeth as soft as snow.

Cook inside a volcano,
Best seen on a snowy afternoon.

Stacey Scott (8)
Exeter Junior School

The Moon

The full moon is like a silver cloak.
Like a white eye staring at us.
Like a rotating wheel going round us.
Like a cookie; all bumpy.

The changing moon is like a smashed glass.
Like the top of a lamp post bending.
Like a boomerang hovering like a glider
Staying as still as a statue.

Hayden Close (8)
Exeter Junior School

The Cupboard

(In the style of Miroslav Holub)

Go and open the cupboard,
Maybe you can see a cottage
Of sweets with bubblegum
Rain that melts the soft chocolate.

Go and open the cupboard
Maybe you can see a dream city,
With tower blocks tickling the stars.

Go and open the cupboard,
Maybe you can see a flying dog
With wings as white as clouds,
That sway in the sky.

Go and see through the cupboard
You might have a big surprise!
It is empty!

Maja Boric (9)
Exeter Junior School

How To Be a Good Friend

Being a good friend is caring and sharing
You need to always be there for them
If you want to be a better friend
Never drive them round the bend
Share their company
Help them work don't go berserk
Play games with them, stay together
Best friends, forever.

Christina Mangin (11)
Exeter Junior School

The Moon

The full moon is like a gigantic
Football gliding down the pitch,
Like a white wheel drifting
Down to Earth.

The half moon is like a banana,
Like an elf's sharp, pointy ear
Tickling the glittering stars,
Like a large smiling mouth
Singing to God above.
Like an enormous bow and arrow
Shooting the dark clouds like Robin Hood,
Like a swinging hammock floating
Down to Earth as fast as a jet.

Celine Pearson (8)
Exeter Junior School

View From My Window

I can smell pizza that has just been burning,
And little children in the school that have just been learning,
I can hear growling dogs,
With their owners throwing logs,
I can feel smooth cars,
With people coming out of stinky bars,
I can smell lovely food
And see a cool dude,
I can see a colourful kite,
With a plane about to go into flight.

Nicky Backo (10)
Exeter Junior School

Recipe For A Mythical Creature

Add:
A head as bright and big as a circle
Eyes as dusty as coal,
A mouth as red as lipstick,
Teeth as blue as a colouring pencil
And a nose as wet as water.

Mix:
A body like a pink trunk of a tree,
Legs that are white as the moon and
So bendy like a T-shirt,
Wings as purple as the sunset.

Stir in:
A tail as white as snow,
The skin so scaly and soft like cotton wool.

Jade Linnell (8)
Exeter Junior School

View From My Window

I look at the moonlight in the night,
I am looking at the stars tonight,
Please may I see -
Not a man with a spot,
Or not a cat that's lost the plot,
Please may I see a lollipop lady
Stopping the traffic not children playing
In the attic,
They might be playing with the rackets,
Please may I see Mother Nature in the wild,
Because she is looking
After the caring child.

Megan Sherlock (9)
Exeter Junior School

The Moon

The full moon is like a round button staring at the world.
Like a shiny dinner plate gazing out at space.
Like a silver ball spinning silently.
Like a giant wheel rolling down the hill.

The changing moon is like a big smile with lipstick on it.
Like a large smile singing up at God.
Like a bow and arrow shooting in the dark like Robin Hood.
Like a banana curved like a dead flower.

Stephanie Bradshaw (9)
Exeter Junior School

The Moon

The full moon is like a shiny marble bouncing up and down.
Like a huge headlight looking at the earth.
Like a round dinner plate spinning all around.
Like a round eye staring at the sun.
The changing moon is like an upset mouth turned upside down.
Like a great boomerang going upside down
And straight like a bow going in different directions.
Like the trigger of a gun going back and forward.

Sam Murray (9)
Exeter Junior School

How To Be A Good Cousin

C herish the times when you are together.
O utdoors are the best to play.
U se your ears and listen to what they say.
S ay goodbye when they leave.
I f when they go you start to grieve.
N ow don't start to cry or they will have you
wrapped around their little finger.

Shona Flynn (11)
Exeter Junior School

How To Be A Good Celebrity

You have to look gorgeous,
speak so posh.

Wear the best clothes that you can,
possibly buy.

Don't chip your long, gorgeous nails.

Keep dying your long, shiny hair,
don't cut it.

If you want to be a good celebrity
I suggest you follow my rules.

Chloe Williams (9)
Exeter Junior School

How To Be A Gorilla

Eat lots of bananas,
you will grow lots of hair.

Then you eat the nits
of the other gorillas.

Then eat more bananas
then you will be turning into a gorilla.

You will dance around
and have a rampage in the zoo.

Lee McIntyre (11)
Exeter Junior School

How To Be A Brilliant Friend

Always tell them where you are going.
Never leave them alone and always keep them company.
Keep them talking and always play with them.
My best friend Kayleigh, she is so strict.
She never leaves me alone, to have a cup of tea.

Samantha Henderson (11)
Exeter Junior School

View From My Window

Sitting by the window, listen to the birds sing,
Creep up and listen to the phone ring.

Looking up the tree to see the bee,
Listen to the sea.

Looking at the flower, to give you power,
Eating the chips and licking your lips,
I feel the breeze on my knees.

Samantha McSherry (10)
Exeter Junior School

View From My Window

I can see people walking, tasting the scrumptious chicken nuggets,
The beautiful meadow being destroyed by the terrifying machines,
Tasting the tangy air makes me petrified. It continues to be polluted,
The dogs howling and roaring won't let me sleep,
Will someone give me a solution?

Ivo Silva (10)
Exeter Junior School

View From My Window

I can hear the screeching of the cars,
I can see howling from the dog,
I can feel the gentle breeze rustling through the leaves,
I can smell the car fumes, smoke that makes us all choke.

Raith Phillips (9)
Exeter Junior School

Recipe For A Mythical Creature

Mix
Lava to make the head,
Some ketchup to make the head red.
Add
Some bark from a tree for the neck.
Fry
An orang-utan's voice box.
Mix
A kickboxer's muscles,
Add
A great white shark's tail,
Mix
Some Tudor blood to make it cruel,
Finally add some vampire teeth.

Andrew Moncaster (9)
Exeter Junior School

The Door

Go and open the door,
Maybe you can see a haunted football pitch,
With scary ghosts flying around the pitch,
Go and open the door,
Maybe you can see a massive swimming pool,
Smelly fish flying in the air,
Go and open the door,
Maybe you will see a dream city,
Tiny houses as small as people.

Go and open the door
You might smell the fresh air.

Michael Paul England (8)
Exeter Junior School

The Moon

The full moon is like a shiny eye staring everywhere,
Like an invisible ghost strolling through walls,
Like a spinning wheel swirling hoops,
Like a haunted marble rolling about,
The changing moon is like a smooth banana
Laying in a bowl of fruit,
Like a jolly smile smiling at everyone,
Like a Viking longboat floating on water,
Like a rabbit's ear flopping about,
The half moon is like an eyebrow blinking at you,
Like a bow and arrow racing across the world,
Like a segment of an orange squirting
Orange juice at you.

Vicky Black (9)
Exeter Junior School

The Moon

The full moon is like a shiny ball,
Spinning around the Earth,
Like a satellite searching space,
Like a white sky gleaming in the dark,
Like a headlight searching for a star.

The changing moon is like a swaying
Swing drifting gently,
Like a thumbprint in the blue sky,
Like a smiling mouth on a clown.

Nicole McMeekin (9)
Exeter Junior School

The Window

Go and look through the window,
Maybe there's a candy house with melting chocolate
Trickling slowly.

Go and look through the window,
Maybe there's candy land with
Marshmallow grass swaying in the wind.

Go open the window
Maybe there's a unicorn
Spreading its glitter over the city,
Go open the window
Let the magic in.

Eleanor Rogerson (9)
Exeter Junior School

Mythical Creature

Wings as red as blood,
Head as blue as water,
Teeth as sharp as a knife,
Feet as shiny as tin foil,
Legs as long as a train,
Eyes as red as fire,
Tail as short as a car,
Nose as green as grass,
Arms as long as an aeroplane,
Cook in an outdoor kitchen
For ten minutes.

Sandro Moreira (9)
Exeter Junior School

Recipe For A Mythical Creature

Add a body as fat as a balloon,
Eyes as white as a blank piece of paper,
Big and bulgy legs,
Simmer wings shaped like a fork,
Toss in excellent hearing from a mile away.

Cook in a hot bubble bath for 20 years,
Then serve.

Danielle McDowell (8)
Exeter Junior School

Mythical Creature

He has a great head as
Fat as a space hopper,
The wings are as smooth as
A butterfly's.
Add the body as tiny as an ants,
Cool in the North Pole for 10 minutes.

Georgia McLaughlin (8)
Exeter Junior School

Recipe For A Mythical Creature

Add the head of a fierce lion,
Teeth as sharp as a shark,
Claws as sharp as Godzila,
Fry a nose as pointy as a witches,
Eyes are as fierce as a tiger's
Cool in an iceberg for one week.

Lee Holmes (8)
Exeter Junior School

Recipe For A Mythical Creature

Add a head as tall as a giraffe's neck,
A nose as long as an elephant's truck,
Stir eyes like coal burning
And a tail as short as a stegosaurus,
Cool with skin as slithery as a snake
And wings as enormous as an eagle,
Heat with teeth as sharp as a vampire's fangs.

Tom Redden (9)
Exeter Junior School

The Witches

The witches flew in the air,
Jumping and turning everywhere,
The witches flew over every house,
Casting spells on every mouse.

Run little children into bed,
Before the witches chop off your head,
Dark and evil is their way,
Death and evil before you lay.

Most evil of them all,
The old witch in a long dark shawl,
Run across the graveyard, go,
Cutting through the lake you row.

Dark night is creeping to a close,
The witches tell new light by their nose,
Witches crawl into their lair,
Once again the night becomes bare.

Light kills witches, quick to death,
Soon witches shall draw their last breath,
The witches let out a mighty roar,
Who knows who is standing at your door . . .

Chloe Binley (10)
Great Addington CE Primary School

One Night

One cold and frosty night,
They told us 'Leave your home!
It's no longer yours to own,
Hurry up, do not take long,
When we come back, you had better be gone.'

Confusion, tension, sadness and fear,
Losing our homes and everything dear,
With only a few items to pack,
We knew we could never come back.

What do we pack?
Food to eat, toys to comfort,
Clothes for warmth,
Memories happy, future sad,
All packed up in a carrier bag.

We are on our way,
The door has closed,
Nowhere to stay,
No time to play,
All in the dark and all alone,
Nowhere for us to call home.

Rebecca Gibbard-Walker (9)
Great Addington CE Primary School

Feelings

Feelings are inside my heart and mind,
I can't seem to separate them I find.
Sadness is an emotion inside of me,
When I'm sad chocolate seems to be the only key.

I'm happy pretty much every day,
Especially when it's my birthday.
I'm angry, frustrated, and sometimes mad,
But that's no excuse for me being bad.

Annabelle Chang (11)
Great Addington CE Primary School

Green Shoes

Oh, idilly, widdly, fiddly, doo
Can you feel the wiggly too?
See the green shoes go and prance
While they did a lovely dance.

They skipped and flipped and twirled around
Feel the green shoes hit the ground
Leprechauns and mushrooms too,
Can you smell the rabbit stew?

In a meadow a clover grew
Hear the cow shout out with glee 'Moo'
Have a pat and have a pan
Just like old Saint Patrick ran.

Oh idlly, widdly, fiddly, doo
Can you feel the wiggly too?
See the green shoes go and prance,
While they did a lovely dance.

Elliot Gudge (10)
Great Addington CE Primary School

Tag

I ran,
The adrenaline pumped through my body,
I accelerated,
As my feet briskly tapped the hard tarmac,
I saw the shadow, sneak up behind,
'Run, run,' my mind screamed,
As my feet raped the floor,
'Faster, faster' my body urged,
Then he touched me like a bullet.
Tag.

David Page (9)
Great Addington CE Primary School

Morning

Tiny rustles in a hedge
Cockerels crowing
Eagle perches on a cliff ledge
Gentle zephyr blowing.

Sun rising slowly up
Sea sparkles bright
Hot chocolate in a cup
Flying red kite.

Sparkling snow drift
Shining sunlight
High flying swift
Disappeared has night.

Laura Miller (11)
Great Addington CE Primary School

Who Is There?

Dancing figures,
Dancing dead,
Spinning,
Twirling,
All around my bed,
Hide me,
Guide me,
Away from them,
Whispering,
But shouting,
Reminding me,
Of them.

Alex Page (11)
Great Addington CE Primary School

Kitten

Watching, waiting, listening, staring,
Tail swishing, eyes glaring,
Playing with a ball of string,
Listening to the blackbirds sing,
Fluffy ears, bright pink nose,
Soft black fur and padded toes,
A cuddly ball that's full of fun,
That leaps, purrs and scuttles whilst on the run,
Watching, waiting, listening, staring,
Tail swishing, eyes glaring.

Jessie Waterfield (11)
Great Addington CE Primary School

My Mummy

She's a pink flower dancing in the wind,
She's a first-aid box that's always there,
She's the sun that never goes down,
She's a lamb just born,
She's a pink milkshake with chocolate flakes,
She's a brain that's always thinking.

Christopher Fry (9)
Great Addington CE Primary School

My Cat

My cat is hairy,
When she gets angry it's scary,
When she is loud, you get wary,
Her mother was called Mary.

Mark Hall (11)
Great Addington CE Primary School

One Night

Voices shout,
Bodies shiver,
Eyes crying,
Hands quiver,
The night, one night,
Our lives were ruined.

We're walking,
Go back,
No talking,
Keep going,
The night, one night,
Our lives were ruined.

Hands shaking,
Spirits low,
Feet aching,
Progress slow,
The night, one night,
Our lives were ruined.

No return?
Not now.
Coming back?
Somehow.
The night, one night.
Our lives were ruined.

Charlotte Evans (11)
Great Addington CE Primary School

My Dog Ben

He's as furry as my dad's back,
He'll hurry to attack back,
He's as quick as a flash of lightning,
But he is never, never frightening.

Ryan Bruce (10)
Great Addington CE Primary School

The Wind

I hear the wind
Across the plain
A voice so strong
That calls my name.
It's wild like the river
It's warm like the sun
It's here,
This is where I belong.

I hear the wind
The fiery flames
The voice is gone
It's gone again
The world all around me
Is fighting to reign
The blood,
The bones and pain.

Olivia Weatherill (10)
Great Addington CE Primary School

My Mum

My mum is a soft and comfy chair,
She has beautiful long blonde hair,
My mum always keeps the house clean,
She never does need a helping team,
My mum is like a clever computer,
She teaches me like a brilliant tutor,
My mum is really the best,
She is better than all the rest!

Gemma Walker (10)
Great Addington CE Primary School

My Head Teacher

She's a
Fast flowing
Pencil writing
On the table.

A cold ice cube
Dripping on the land

A fast cheetah
Leaping on the sand

A yellow orange leaf
Floating down to the floor.

She's a soft coat swaying
On the door.

Chantèle Height (9)
Great Addington CE Primary School

Antonia

She is a sparkly new dress,
She is a bottle of fizzy Coke but can be a still glass of water,
She is a set of chattering teeth,
She is the brightest light bulb ever,
She is ice cream covered in chocolate sauce,
She is as clever as a computer,
She is a pile of books waiting to be read,
She is as wonderful as a saint,
She is as lovely as a wild flower,
She is as loud as a horn,
She is as funny as a clown,
She is just like a bomb hit our bedroom,
She is my *sister!*

Naomi Brown (10)
Great Addington CE Primary School

Wizard's Duel

Flames flare,
Glitters gleam,
The duel is on,
Do not be seen.

Wands wave,
Sparks fly,
Evil approaching,
Evil die.

Beams flash,
Flickers fizz,
Wizard stumbled,
Bends and missed.

Wands wave,
Sparks fly,
Evil approaching,
Evil die.

Wands flash,
Wizard strikes,
Evil stops,
And cost him his life.

Rhiannon Evans (10)
Great Addington CE Primary School

Spider Haiku

Eight long hairy legs
Round and black bulging belly,
Slowly hunting prey.

Josh Parbery (10)
Great Addington CE Primary School

The Day Of Snow

Cold, white snow,
Sledges sliding down the hill,
Snow is cold,
Snow is freezing,
When snow falls on mud,
It goes soggy and brown,
My fingers go cold on a cold winter's day.

Michael Houseman (7)
Great Addington CE Primary School

Tom Tickled Tiger Tony

Tom tickled Tiger Tony as the teacher taught him,
The tiger that Tom tickled
Tickled the teacher that taught
Tom how to tickle.
But the teacher that taught
Tom how to tickle, tickled
Tom and Tiger Tony.

Thomas York (9)
Great Addington CE Primary School

My Mum

She's a hot chocolate with ice white whipped cream,
She's a cuddly puppy all soft and silk.

A waterbed all snug on an eerie winter night,
She's the summer sun shining on a golden paradise beach,
She's my magical mum.

Cara Marsh (11)
Great Addington CE Primary School

Snowflake

'Snowflake, snowflake tumbling down,
Where will you land?
In the grass or on the pavement?
We will never, never know.

Snow we play in you,
From time to time you come or go,
Have you got big gaps?
Have you got small gaps?

Do you land on rooftops
Or do you land in plants?
How far do you travel?'
'We travel from sunny
And sandy lands and
Snowy and icy lands.'

I love watching snowflakes
Tumbling down from the sky.

Eve Lopez (8)
Gretton Primary School

Winter

The floor is slippery and dangerous,
It is fun to play snowball fights,
Icicles hanging down from rooftops,
Children playing outside,
It is fun to go sledging,
It is fun making snowmen,
Icicles sparkling down,
It is fun at Christmas.

Kimberley Webster (7)
Gretton Primary School

Winter Weather

Snow
Crunchy, slippery
Fun, beautiful, flying,
Fun to play in
Snow.

Ice
Cold, slippery,
Hard, see-through, solid,
Hard as solid stone
Ice.

Winter
Cold, windy
Freezing, stone cold, good,
Full with fun definitely
Winter.

Benjamin Cowley (7)
Gretton Primary School

Snow

S is for smooth snow,
N is for night when snow comes down,
O is for oak tree covered in snow,
W is for wintry snow!

Samuel Branston (7)
Gretton Primary School

Winter Weather

Snow
Heavy, hard
White, soft, slippery
Like a cream carpet
Snow.

Winter
Icy, cold
Biting, blizzards, hailstones
Floating flakes flying
Winter.

Ice
Frozen, thin,
Fun, freezing, skiddy
As solid as a rock,
Ice.

Edward Harris (8)
Gretton Primary School

Winter

Winter is fun, as fun as can be
And I want all the snow for me.
Children throwing snowballs
Moulding them into shape,
Then comes down a lot of snowflakes.
Big snowmen getting higher and higher
And people in their houses by the warm fire.
The snow crackling under my feet
And children that look so sweet.

Steven Allen (8)
Gretton Primary School

A Witch's Brew

Let's bubble and boil a witch's brew
Riches and pearls it will bring to you
First let's mix:

Bat's eyes to make the night rise,
Jelly from an eye to make this potion spy,
Human toes for lots of foes,
Ear wax and a bloody axe,
Rats' tails so he can break from jails,
Hailstones and crumbly bones,
If it smells like dead fish and rotten eggs
For long springy legs,
Now it should be bright blood-red and bubbly,
And makes your tummy rumbly,
Now it has turned into a brown juicy,
Chicken on a stylish silver platter,
In our cauldron.

Paige Haworth (10)
Gretton Primary School

Kennings Grandfather Clock

Hallway-keeper,
Night-sleeper,
Hour-donger,
Huge-clocker,
Number-watcher,
Tick-tocker,
Hand-clicker,
Face-winker,
House-owner,
Ticking-moaner,
Long-swinger,
Tick-tocker,
Never-stopper.

Naomi Palmer (11)
Gretton Primary School

My First Pony!

Dancer was my first,
As white as silver snow,
She moved like the wind,
Hooves beating like your heart,
She gleamed with a glossy coat,
Moved swiftly like a boat.

She paraded, showing her silky surface,
Dashing and dancing, prancing all day,
Darts did she when jumping,
Galloped in a herd of friends,
Cantered with speed round a course,
When she was wild she jumped gorse.

Her silver coat shimmered in the dew,
As soft as silk or satin blankets,
Her mane and tail flowed like streaks of corn,
She bounded through patchwork fields,
Golden thread is the straw revealed.

She pawed the ground with anger,
Mud flew like a water shower,
She carefully moved to the floor,
Then she rolled, and rolled again,
She was extremely naughty but I'm not stern.

All my life, as long as I live I'll love her
Dancer was so sweet and sound,
But now my feet touch the ground.

Sophie-Jo McKinnon (8)
Gretton Primary School

Kennings Cat

Claw-scratcher,
Mouse-catcher,
Fur-licker,
Tail-flicker,
Wet-kisser,
Angry-hisser,
Milk-drinker,
Water-sinker,
Sleepy-waker,
Meat-taker,
Wall-prowler,
Moon-howler,
Bird-biter,
Dog-fighter,
Tree-climber,
Fish-finder,
Kitten-cuddler,
Ball of wool-muddler,
Fish-lover,
Fur-cover.

Ailish Tait (10)
Gretton Primary School

Great White Shark

S is for sea, the sea floats around,
H is for harmful sharks hurt fish,
A is for alive, sharks are alive,
R is for race, the sharks race to find fish,
K is for keep, keep that fish for lunch,
S is for seaweed, that's a weed underwater.

L is for lie, sharks always lie,
I is for island, the sharks swim round an island,
V is for violent, sharks are violent,
E is for Edward, a possible shark name.

Jamie McEwan (8)
Gretton Primary School

Seasons

Winter is spotless, white all over the ground,
Winter is when people have snowball fights,
Winter is when they touch the snow with their furry gloves,
Winter is when you get your sleigh out.

Summer is when you play out with your friends,
Summer is when you play with your sandpit,
Summer is when you don't wrap up warm,
Summer is warm, not like winter,
Summer is when you play in the swimming pool.

Spring is when you look at the pretty flowers,
Spring is when the trees sway from side to side,
Spring is when you pick lovely flowers,
Spring is when the flowers grow,
Spring is lovely.

Autumn is when the trees are pretty,
Autumn is when you look at the brown dropping leaves,
Autumn is when you play in the leaves,
Autumn is when you climb trees,
Autumn is when you brush the crunchy leaves.

Lucy Harrison (8)
Gretton Primary School

Friends And Family

Friends are nice to be with when you're alone,
Our parents are loving and caring,
If I am hurt, my friends always help me,
My best friend is always by my side,
My family is a kind of guard that always keeps me safe,
My parents are one of those parents
Who yells at me but still loves me,
I love my friends and family.

Niamh Tait (7)
Gretton Primary School

All Seasons

Summer
Sunshine blazing in the air
Eating ice pops on the beach
Swimming in the salty sea
Paddling in the paddling pool
Playing games in the park.

Autumn
Crunchy leaves golden and brown
Trees shaking in whistling wind
Leaves flying everywhere
Squirrels collecting nuts for their winter feast
Brushing up all different colours of leaves.

Winter
Glittering snow shimmering on the ground
Freezing frost spreading around
Red roses in the garden
Gloves on tight so no bitten fingers
Pretty patterns on windows.

Spring
Young baby animals being born
Planting fresh seeds and brushing soil on top
Roses growing thorns
Having picnics on a sunny day
Vegetables growing all the time.

Grace Clark (7)
Gretton Primary School

Things To Do With Winter

Winter
Frosty, freezing,
Snowy, slippery, cold
Fun and very beautiful
Winter.

Snow
Icy, glittering
Shiny, soft, mushy
You're able to skid,
Snow.

Frost
Thin, wet
Delicate, graceful, patterned
Frost is frozen snow,
Frost.

Jack Haworth (7)
Gretton Primary School

My Dolphin

Roxana, my dolphin, is extremely bold but sometimes quite shy,
My dolphin Roxana is the most elegant dolphin in the ocean,
She is an amusing companion to have around!
Roxana is extremely talented and can do backstroke and
front crawl!
When Roxana swims around you can see her glistening
in the salty sea,
She is a very cheeky dolphin!
My dolphin dives from dawn until dusk and swoops down
To catch a big fish,
Roxana is the best dolphin in the whole world!

Eleanor Greenan (8)
Gretton Primary School

Winter

Winter
Cold, icy,
Frozen, delicate, bare,
It's carpeted with snow,
Winter.

Snow
Flakes, fun,
Soft, light, fragile,
Trapped in the glittering,
Snow.

Frost
Crunchy, white,
Sparkle, sprinkled, fresh,
Clutched onto the grass,
Frost.

Cold
Nipped, biting,
Bitter, glistening, wintry,
Nipping our little noses,
Cold.

Melissa Dolby (8)
Gretton Primary School

Winter Is . . .

Sparkling
Spectacular
Silver
And special.

Frosty
Frozen
It's fragile
Firm.

Lauren Smith (8)
Gretton Primary School

The Animal From Orbit

Stingey, the stingey, what is the stingey?
I have not a clue,
Is it thin? Is it fat? Does it turn into a bat
Or even do acrobatics?
Stingey, the stingey, what is the stingey?
My mother would like to know,
Is it chunky or slimy or pulls rude faces behind me?
Stingey, the stingey, what is the stingey?
My father would like to hear,
Is it here? Is it there? Is it here? Is it there?
It's kind of sort of everywhere.
Stingey, the stingey, what is the stingey?
My brother would like to see,
Does it have tears made of sparkling silk
Or even drink milk? Whatever can it be?
Stingey, the stingey, what is the stingey?
We're all in despair,
Does it have hair or is it bare
Or can it even say there?
Stingey, the stingey, what is the stingey?
Oh, I give up!

Rebecca Wymant (9)
Gretton Primary School

Winter

The snow drops glistening in the moonlight sparkling in the day,
Trees cracking as they sway in the wind,
Footprints paced all over the snow, all shapes and sizes,
The smell of Sunday roast coming from a steamed up window,
Out in the cold biting air, snowflakes falling from the sky,
Little clouds of coldness, ball of ice,
Wet gloves from snowball fights and picking up snow.

Sophie Redman-Baber (8)
Gretton Primary School

Kennings Axe

Tree-cutter
Wood-splitter
Blood-maker
Sword-taker
Shield-cracker
Skull-whacker
Thunder-striker
Gore-liker
Sharp-slicer
Brain-dicer
Mind-shaker
Bone-breaker
Barbaric-walker
Short-talker
Violent-killer
Blood-spiller.

Aiden Swan (11)
Gretton Primary School

My Dog Twotone

My dog Twotone looks
Spotty
Sweet

My dog Twotone feels
Cute
Cuddly

My dog Twotone smells
Clean
Refreshing.

Hayley Binder (8)
Gretton Primary School

Kennings Lion

Zebra-pacers,
Wildebeest-breakers.

Night-hunters,
Group-grunters.

Human-haters,
Violent-maters.

Meat-eaters,
Day-sleepers.

Danger-makers,
Peace-takers.

Young-fighters,
Powerful-biters.

Young leavers,
Cub-teasers.

Tree-climbers,
Bone-grinders.

King of the plains.

Tom Pilgrem (9)
Gretton Primary School

Winter

W hite, soft snow icy cold,
I play and roll in it,
N ever stop throwing snowballs,
T iny snowflakes falling on kitty's nose,
E ars covered by warm winter hats,
R hea the cat, rolling in the snow.

S oft white blanket over the lawn,
N oses rosy-red,
O utside you see children playing,
W ow! Snow is great to play in!

Sophie Ferguson (7)
Gretton Primary School

Kennings School

Bell-ringers
Homework-bringers
Rule-makers
Model-breakers
Crumb-moppers
Scissor-droppers
Work-haters
Book-raters
Ball-kickers
Friend-trickers
Ruler-snappers
Sony-rappers
Nose-pickers
Finger-lickers
Story-writers
Poem-reciters
Teacher-puzzlers
Drink-guzzlers
Trouser-tearers
Bag-wearers.

Nathan Cowley (9)
Gretton Primary School

Kennings Owl

Wing-flapper
Sky-glider
Forest-watcher
Night-hunter
Powerful-howler
Mice-catcher
Great-lander
Wise-flyer
Talons-grabber
Eagle-hater.

Rachel Jackson (9)
Gretton Primary School

Night Prowler

A flash of burgundy and white,
A silent hunter stalking prey,
Chicken thief, wild howler, a padding prowler,
Swift as the wind with a moments notice,
Deadly as a knife, a devil, a hunter's highest level.

Rabbit killer, turkey stealer,
Hole digger, farmer tricker, cub licker,
Silky fur of blood-red and ebony-black,
Eyes of soft hazel showing adventure,
Paws like smooth leather covered with mud.

Looks like a killer in its moods,
But graceful mother she is.

Fox.

Emily Arnold (0)
Gretton Primary School

Volcano

Like a solid steel wall
Colossal, danger, fierce,
Rumbles when it erupts
Huge, risky, wild,
A devil from the sky,
Jumbo, threat, brutal,
Lava tips of the crater,
Volcano!

Anthony Watts (8)
Gretton Primary School

Why? Why? Why?

Why? Why? Why?
I wonder through and through,
Why? Why? Why?
I didn't know what to do,
Why? Why? Why?
I couldn't get to bed,
Why? Why? Why?
She fell upon her head,
Why? Why? Why?
She climbed so high,
Why? Why? Why?
She said goodbye,
Crash!
Falling,
Swaying fast,
A steep *crash!*
In a deep sleep, never coming back,
She *fell!*
Whistling in the breeze,
A musty, damp smell filling the air with guilt,
The tree stood tall,
I think of her flexible kick, her sporty clothes,
She was cold and tall like the tree,
Then I saw him, the killer, the
Tree!

Hollie Downing (10)
Gretton Primary School

Kennings Clown

Face-painter,
Pretend-fainter.

Pie-thrower,
Trumpet-blower.

Comical-dancer,
Amusing-prancer.

Car-driver,
Water-diver.

Walking-waddler,
Laughing-toddler.

Tightrope-walker,
Ridiculous-talker.

Car-breaker,
Unicycle-racer.

Ball-juggler,
Scarlet nosed-smuggler.

Squirting-flower,
Faking-cowerer.

Stilt-strider,
Tandem-rider.

Caravan-lurker,
Circus-worker.

Clown!

William Grisley (10)
Gretton Primary School

Old Shark

A vicious shark,
Ancient and ashen,
In the crystal ocean,
In his spectacular mansion.

King of the sea,
With his sharp, spiky teeth,
Hunting sneaky squirming fish,
In the coral reef.

Filled with hatred,
At the sight of man,
With their sharp, shiny weapons,
Getting ready to turn him into ham.

What's that beautiful smell?
He's checking it out,
Hey what - the
Something's hooked him on his snout.

It's sucking him out of the water,
Onto a funny thing,
Here comes a tagger,
Ouch! That did sting.

Phew! He's let him back,
Into the water,
When he thought
He'd be slaughtered.

A vicious shark,
Ancient and ashen,
In the crystal ocean,
In his spectacular mansion.

James Stupples (11)
Gretton Primary School

The Mouse

Squeaks like a rusty axle,
Moves like a thunderbolt smashing into the ground,
As soft as a warm blanket,
As small as a tiny ant scuffling along the ground,
Climbs like a monkey swinging between the bars,
Gnaws a nut like a knife,
Makes burrows as deep as craters,
Nibbles cheese like a JCB digging up the ground,
Its eyes are like stars shining in the sky,
Its tail's like a helicopter blade spinning round and round,
Its ears are gigantic and spiky like a mountain top,
Its tail's as long as a ball of string.

Tom Grisley (9)
Gretton Primary School

A Nonsense Poem

I am a nonsense fella,
My name is Bella,
And my bed is made out of socks,
My wallpaper is made of chickenpox,
I live in melted ice cream
And I dream of a football team,
It rains poodles and noodles,
My money is named Googals,
I'm a really good friend,
But I have to say goodbye,
Because it is the end.

Josie Downing (8)
Gretton Primary School

Kennings School Teachers

Whistle blowers
Ball throwers
Coffee drinkers
Homework thinkers
Work setters
Tea getters
Work explainers
Netball trainers
Quick tickers
Football kickers
Test raters
Hometime waiters.

Jack Irwin (10)
Gretton Primary School

Kennings Dog

Tail chaser,
Mongrel racer,
Food pincher,
Loud whinger,
Mad howler,
Thunderous growler,
Large scratcher,
Toy snatcher,
Mouse discoverer,
Biscuit lover.

Matthew Webster (9)
Gretton Primary School

Autumn

The warm autumn season
After summer before winter
Warm season passed cold, crisp season ahead.

Horse chestnut trees sprouting little green
Balls with sharp spikes.

The great oaks foliage rapidly decreasing of
Its crimson and golden-brown leaves.

I see grey squirrels collecting food for the cold
Winter season ahead.

I like autumn because of its beautiful colours.

Grace Serena-Heaton (9)
Gretton Primary School

Numbers

One old owl,
Two tired tigers,
Three thin thieves,
Four fashionable fathers,
Five fat fish,
Six sensible sharks,
Seven scientific servants,
Eight embarrassed elephants,
Nine naughty navigators,
Ten trustworthy twins.

Leigh-Anne Bell (8)
Gretton Primary School

The Mountain

The mountain stands up in the sky
Higher than the birds can fly,
At the top of the mountain, it is so cold,
The mountain is big and bold,
It's mostly rough
And is tough
The rugged rocks are extremely bumpy,
From the distance they look lumpy,
The mountain.

Thomas Walker (9)
Gretton Primary School

Snowflakes

Snowflakes, snowflakes,
Fluttering all around.

Snowflakes, snowflakes,
Falling to the ground.

As cold as ice,
As cold as snow.

If you like it,
Crouch down low.

Katherine Shaw (8)
Hackleton Primary School

Winter Wonderland

Snow as white as wool
Snowflakes as delicate as snakeskin,
Snowmen standing in a snowstorm,
Tiny bits of snow fall on my nose.

Jonathan Roy Young (8)
Hackleton Primary School

My Lost Dog

I left my dog out in the frost
Then it snowed and now he's lost.
He's only little so he can't see
Over the snow like you and me.

He's probably down a huge drain
Scrambling up and down again.
He came back at ten to three
And he'd been hiding under a really tall tree.

I wrapped him in a blanket to try to keep him warm,
But he wriggled and wriggled like a baby just born.
I was so glad to see him because I missed him so
After I had dried him, his coat began to glow.

I never want to lose him again,
For he is my precious dog Ben.

Robyn Dickin (8)
Hackleton Primary School

The Song Of The Snake

I sit or lay
Waiting for my prey.

When my prey is in sight
I grab it and squeeze it tight.

I grab it by the head
Just to make sure it's dead.

Then I take it to my hole,
And swallow it whole.

Such a tasty treat
Are you sure it's not meat?

Joshua Clark (9)
Hackleton Primary School

Rugby

I love rugby
And I go and watch the games
My grandad has a special seat
Which always is the same.

We watch Northampton Saints
And they are very grand
They've won so many games
They built a brand new stand.

Some of the Saints players
Play for the English team
And they beat the Aussies
Which made my auntie's scream.

Rugby's never boring
I like it day and night
I especially like the games
When they all get in a fight.

My uncle's played rugby
And so did my stepdad
But they are all now too old
Though they were not once too bad.

I play games of rugby
I play in Pocket Park
We play all through the summer
Even when it's dark.

The only thing that's bad
Are the scars over the years
My uncle is quite handsome
Apart for his cauliflower ears.

The ball is a funny shape
The goalposts are quite high
But it's far better than football
Where they all dance about and cry.

So I will always be a rugby fan
The game is the bestest ever
Rugby fans don't fight and boo
That's because they're clever.

Jago Billings (9)
Hackleton Primary School

Dogs!

Big, small
Short and tall
Chase cats
Sit on mats
Chew on slippers
Eat your knickers
Munch on meat
While we eat
Bad dog!
Why aren't you as good as a hog?
Sleep in baskets
Not shopping baskets
Run up the wall
Then they fall
Fluffy fur
Some people say 'Eurgh!'
Roll in mud
Break your studs.

Are dogs really like this?

Sophie Cook (9)
Hackleton Primary School

Fatty Puffs!

Fatty puffs are big and round,
They look just like a ball,
They stuff themselves with lemonade,
And cake but that's not all.

'Cause fatty puffs are . . .

Chocolate scoffers
Marvellous meal eaters
Hourly nappers
Slow walkers
Splendid sleepers
Dozy dreamers
Jolly jokers.

They're the happiest people around!

Emilie Biggs (9)
Hackleton Primary School

Joseph

Chocolate scavenger
Pet lover
TV watcher
Football player
Bike rider
Hockey liker
Brilliant swimmer
Lemonade licker
Sweet eater
Milkshake maker
I am Joseph.

Joseph Porter (9)
Hackleton Primary School

The Roaring Lion

In the jungle far away,
There is a lion,
A lion near a tree,
Which roars at sight
People fight,
People kill him,
To eat him and everything
This ain't right.
We shouldn't fight,
The lion roars and roars
The lion roars in death,
As people eat him,
Just for food,
The lion roars again and again.

Chloe Spokes (9)
Hackleton Primary School

Eating Healthily

When you are hungry and feel like you want to eat,
Pick up a piece of fruit, it's better than a sweet,
If you eat a load of candy,
A trip to the dentist could come in handy,
An apple, banana, orange and a pear,
Are better than sweets, they can get stuck in your hair,
Now every day you should eat,
Fruit, a plant and a small piece of meat,
To keep healthy,
Whether you're a bit poor or you're wealthy,
Fish is known to make you smart,
It works better than treacle tarts,
Dairy products make your bones grow strong,
Your 5 a day will make you healthy and live for long.

Hannah Bradley (10)
Hackleton Primary School

Untitled

8.55am and the whistle blows
We all line up and in we go!
Coats off, books out, sitting with our pens,
But there's no need today
It's day ten!

Day ten, art day, fun, fun, fun!
All get into our groups
And the fun has begun.

The cameras are clicking,
The mosaics are sticking
Some are painting
But everyone's making

3 hours have passed
Time goes so fast
It's time to go for lunch
But we are still happy
Because we are so lucky
We all have a hot dog to munch.

Sophie Acharya (9)
Hackleton Primary School

The Room Of Feelings

The room of feeling is silent but alive,
The room of feeling is warm but not comfortable,
The room of feeling is light and yet dark,
The room of feeling is cold but warm,
The room of feeling is wonderful but weird,
The room of feeling is mysterious but magical,
The room of feeling is changing as we speak.

Hannah Collier (9)
Hackleton Primary School

England's World Cup Triumph

England's way to the final
Was easy for a while,
Until it came to France,
Where they had a chance.

We were ready for the semi-final,
But we had to wait a while,
Until the score came through,
When we had nothing to do.

We were through to the final,
But we were against a hard rival,
We had to play the home side,
Who would give us a hard ride.

Australia were expected to win,
Would we leave them in a spin?
The game was nigh
And our hopes were high.

We were drawing - thanks to Wilkinson
And a try from Robinson,
In extra time Wilkinson took his chance,
He kicked the ball and we watched it dance.

The final whistle was blown,
Australia were left on their own,
England let out a massive cheer,
And many people shed a tear.

Charles Cleland (9)
Hackleton Primary School

Bonfire Night

On Bonfire Night the fireworks go bang
And the bonfire crackles in the dark
As the moon comes up and the church bells ring
The children waited in the park.

The sky turns blue and silver and gold
My toes, my fingers and my nose gets cold
Toffee apples, candyfloss, marshmallows on a stick
With all these good things, I hope I don't get sick.

The night gets late so it's time to go home
We have all had more fun than we ever have known
We snuggle in bed and dream of what fun
We have had with my sister, my dad and my mum.
And *me!*

Jessica Bradley (9)
Hackleton Primary School

The Beach

On the beach it is lots of fun,
On the beach there's lots of sun,
On the beach you can catch a tan,
But you might need a mini fan!
On the beach there's lots of sea
And when you go home have some warm tea.

Joshua Markham (9)
Hackleton Primary School

Rugby Players

Jason the one that plays for Sale,
Runs just like fast falling hail,
The Aussies try but catch him never,
'Cause he runs just faster than ever.

Martin's the captain you have to admit,
He never likes to see anyone hit,
So when he saw Jonny with a pain in his shoulder,
He must have been as still as a boulder,
But Jonny said, 'I won't stay in bed,
I'll carry on playing though there's an ache in my head.'

Jonny the hero of them all,
Scored an excellent winning drop goal,
The England supporters cried,
'Hooray for Jonny, you Aussies'll be pied.'

But we must not forget young big Ben,
The winger's important as any of them,
All though wingers are meant to be small,
Ben is quite big and I'd say he's quite tall.

Emilie Biggs (9)
Hackleton Primary School

Colours

Multicoloured the colours of coral,
As green is the colour of sorrel,
Red the colour of blood,
Brown the colour of water in a flood,
Fiery-orange the colour of a flame,
The sun is orange - exactly the same,
Everywhere you look you see colour,
We live in a world of colour.

Peter Instrell (10)
Hackleton Primary School

Be Scared

In the dark,
A monster prowls,
Ready to pounce on his prey.
He creeps around,
With no sound,
Echoing on his way.

Thump, thump, thump,
Go his feet prowling along his way.
Bump, bump, bump,
Go his feet through the hard worked day.

He opens a door,
And pounces proudly,
Upon his new prey.
Massacred boys,
And slaughtering girls,
He prowls along his way.

Simran Duhra (10)
Hackleton Primary School

I'm Frightened

A spider is in my bed
    Scary!
A robber's at the window
    Freaky!
A monster is near me
    I'm frightened!
An ogre is coming up the stairs,
    I'm nervous!
I cannot get to sleep
    I'm restless!

Jamie Wilby (10)
Hackleton Primary School

Yellow

Yellow to me means happy,
Yellow is summer,
The blossomed trees,
The colourful flowers,
All the leaves,
Yellow is for joy,
Yellow is for the sand,
Yellow, yellow,
Yellow is for the daffodils that grow,
Yellow is everywhere,
Yellow is the sun,
Yellow is for the desert,
Yellow is for the pyramids,
Yellow is for the creators.

Callum McDonogh (5)
Hackleton Primary School

Wolf

In the woods a wolf appears
Hunting for the caribou
Night and day
Day and night
Starving for some meat.

In its prime
He fills his belly
Yet for another week
No food is needed
But still he hunts.

Jessica Facer (9)
Hackleton Primary School

My Granny, The Big Kid

My granny is really hip and hop
She's really into rock and pop
She rocks the streets and rocks the town
She moves her hands up and moves her hands down
She cracks up with laughter when she sees others dance
She's rocked round the world and she's rocked in France.

My granny plays for the England rugby side
When she was hit by one of The All-Blacks, I don't think she cried
She called the other winger and booted the ball high
She booted it so high it probably went beyond the sky.

In the late sixties my granny was a hippy
If anyone called her goofy names she'd get all lippy
She put on a pink hair band
And hippied through the land and earned a grand.

But now things are normal
And she dresses quite formal
Just hope the secret won't escape
Because she recorded it on a tape.

Cameron Stewart-Mathews (10)
Hackleton Primary School

What Is It?

Slowly moving towards me,
I see it,
Brown,
Fluffy,
It's running at me,
Small, but fierce,
I hear a growl,
Wait, I see it more clearly,
It's . . .
It's my dog!

Georgia Cave (9)
Hackleton Primary School

Pandas

I think pandas are sweet and cuddly,
They're endangered too.
I think it's horrible to cut down trees and kill,
Why do they? Pandas are humans, but just fluffy,
Pandas are my favourite animals, but they're rare to see here.
Pandas are mostly seen in China so please help.
They need their food and shelter,
So please help!

Jasmin Le Bon (9)
Hackleton Primary School

Feelings

When I fall out with Katie
We have an argument
I storm round the corner and hide
Chloe comes and I tell her what I feel
I feel sad, upset and angry
Then tears start rolling down my cheeks.

Justine Sindall (9)
Hackleton Primary School

Hurt

Hurt is when you fall off your bike and bang your head on the wall
Hurt is when you get a graze and sometimes a scar
Sometimes you go to the hospital but you don't always
When you break your arm you do
When you break your leg you do.

Bradley Harradine (9)
Hackleton Primary School

Night-Time

I clench my covers
Look up with fright
I see a shadow
Someone . . . is coming . . . up the stairs
A tear runs down my face
The floor creaks
I fill with shivers
The door opens slightly
Something jumps upon my bed
Argh, help, help, help.

It's my cat
Phew.

William Fall (10)
Hackleton Primary School

Feelings

The feeling of happiness,
Comes in one big wish.
The feeling of fear,
Comes when something horrid is near.
The feeling of sadness,
Comes when you're let all alone.
The feeling of anger,
Comes at just the wrong time.
Feelings are everywhere,
Everywhere you go,
You can't get rid of feelings.

William Barnes (10)
Hackleton Primary School

Red

Red,
The fierce, angry colour,
The colour of blood.
Red,
The mean, nasty colour,
The colour that reminds me of the dead.
Red,
The horrid, sickly colour,
The horror colour.
Red,
The unhappy, disgusting colour,
The colour of the horrid desert sand.
Do I like red?

Rhianna Taylor (10)
Hackleton Primary School

Tick-Tock

Tick-tock
Goes the sound of the clock.

Ding-dong
Goes the sounds of the bell all night long.

Tu-whit tu-whoo
Goes the sound of an owl, or two.

Booo
Goes the sound of a voice, but who?

Argh
'Hello,' goes someone, 'who are you?'

Katie Ramsden (10)
Hackleton Primary School

Mouse Hunt

There's a mouse in the house
Catch it!
Catch it!
Argh
Run little mouse
Run, run, run.

The mouse goes up
And the mouse goes down
Through the tunnels
And through the ground
In the house
In the garden
And even in a crowd.

Through the park
And through the zoo
Ooh, ooh, ooh go the monkeys in the zoo
The lions roar and the snakes go hiss
There goes the mouse
Catch it, catch it.

It's running away through the hours of the day
It gets back to the house
It runs up the stairs
It runs in room after room
Through the kitchen and through the loo
Run little mouse
Run, run, run!
There's a mouse in the house
Catch it, catch it!

Katie O'Sullivan (9)
Hackleton Primary School

How Some People Feel

I feel the anger
I feel alone
The sadness, the grief
I am unknown
I feel so small, no one can see me
Hear me or even say hello
I try and try to let this anger go
But the pain remains inside me.

Hayley Rodgers (9)
Hackleton Primary School

Red

Red - the colour of horror,
The stabbed man,
The fiery underworld,
The reminder of blood,
A devil running round,
Causing havoc through the towns,
Red - the colour of pain.

Tom Pocklington (10)
Hackleton Primary School

White

White is the colour where there's nothing to see,
It will be a quiet place with only white,
White will be the colour of the world,
If only we had more colours we would be OK,
The only way we can see is by colour.
White.

Alice Hendrey (9)
Hackleton Primary School

My Gran

My gran goes to discos
And loves San Francisco
She rides the streets with her skateboard
And she disobeys the Lord
She gives me food that looks like slush
But when she gives me biscuits, life is lush
When she goes to the shop
She tries to play a guitar with a sign saying stop
She has lots of wrinkles
And tries to get them out
I think she's a hippy without a doubt
When she was young she was on the Actimel advert
She's married to a man called Bert
When I was sick and sad
She told me how to say 'Great Grandad'
    That's just my gran!

Alexandra Kerr (10)
Hackleton Primary School

History Lesson

History lesson take me anywhere else, please!
My history teacher smells of cheese.
I hate that boring class,
In all our tests I come last.
It's the worst lesson in the school,
I wish we could do PE instead, that's cool!
Who cares about ancient Rome?
When we learnt about it, I ran home.
So as you can plainly see, I hate history.

Joshua Savage (9)
Hackleton Primary School

Cauldron Cakes

Shell of snail,
Puppy-dog tail,
Slime of slugs,
Plenty of bugs,
A wizard bone,
A telephone,
With crocodile eyes,
And human bow ties,
Frogs' legs,
Washing pegs,
With little duck chicks,
And wooden sticks,
A stick of glue,
The measles (blue),
Bloodstained rats,
Doormat cats,
A fondue set,
Let's place a bet,
Gingerbread men,
A cock and hen,
A very young lad,
The heart of his dad,
Eat this cake,
If you don't want to wake.

Hannah Ward (11)
Hackleton Primary School

Autumn Poem

I saw lots of conkers sitting on the ground
Waiting to be found,
Shiny conkers, smooth as well
I bring a big bucket,
We pick them all day.

I like to jump in the leaves, which are curling when,
They fall down I like,
To jump in the leaves.
All day long I keep doing it,
Again, again, again.

Loads of twigs on the ground,
I take them home and burn them.

Lots of helicopter seeds I find them,
With my mum and dad all day.

Victoria Kingdom (7)
Hackleton Primary School

Watermelons

Watermelons are easy to munch,
As they go *squish* instead of *crunch.*
They're not too bright as you can see,
When they are eaten they go, 'Yippee.'

They only trouble is the pips,
When they are swallowed they do backflips.
This can be solved not by cars,
But by swallowing little backflip bars.

Victoria Moore (11)
Hackleton Primary School

Winter Poem

Winter storm rises loudly,
You can see it proudly.
Snow is fun to play in when it's flying.
Winter is cold and it's freezing,
Flowers dying, snow is flying.
Icy lakes cracking and breaking,
Winter makes people start sneezing.
Hedgehog sleeping in the hedge,
Children playing in the snow.
Snowball thrown through the air,
In the winter nights are longer than days.
Snowmen get built with carrots for their nose,
Stones for their eyes and mouth,
With a hat on their head and a scarf round their neck,
Sticks for hands and arms and stones for buttons.
Last year it was small, we didn't like it.
But winter is fun!

Chris Bull (7)
Hackleton Primary School

Carrots And Jelly

Carrots, carrots, good for your eyes,
The more you eat, the more you sigh.
The more you eat, the more you see,
So eat carrots just like me.

Or perhaps you would prefer,

Jelly, jelly, good for your liver,
The more you eat, the more you quiver.
The more you eat, the more you feel glad,
So eat jelly just like my dad.

Leigh Ramsden (11)
Hackleton Primary School

Spots And Dots

Spots on leopards,
Spots on cheetahs,
Spots and dots on lots of creatures.

Spots on pictures,
Spots on walls,
Spots and dots on lots of balls.

Spots and dots are my favourite things,
But so are poems just like this.

Jade Parmenter (8)
Hackleton Primary School

Roast Dinner

Oh how I hate my smelly Brussels sprouts,
But if I don't eat them my mum really shouts.
With my carrots, parsnip and cauliflower,
I build them up to make a huge tower.
The only thing I hate the most
Is beef and all the stuffing, literally all the roast.
Oh how I really hate my roast dinner,
It will never be to me a big winner.

Hannah Bradley (10)
Hackleton Primary School

Wintertime

Snow falling from the trees
Snow falling from the sky
Water turns into ice
Chucking snowballs
Having fights
Building snowmen
Snow, snow - falling from the trees.

Christopher Keightley (7)
Hackleton Primary School

Best Friends

Best friends are the best,
Sometimes they have the same dress,
And when they have a little fight,
Someone always puts it right.
Going round each other's house,
They're always as quiet as a mouse.
Coming in, going out,
Best friends are always about.
They go to each other's birthday,
Where they all have a dance and a play.
Bringing each other presents from on holiday,
When they just came back last Sunday,
Their friendship will last to the end.

Jessica Ballantyne (8)
Hackleton Primary School

Animals

Puppies' ears are low
Cats' ears are high
Giraffes' necks go to the sky
But I'm just me

Seals live in the sea
Guinea pigs live with me
But I'm just me

Tortoises' legs are short
Alligators' teeth are sharp
But I'm just me.

Liana Wyatt (8)
Hackleton Primary School

Wintertime

Robins singing,
It's a new beginning,
Cold and bitter,
Frozen snow,
Sitting by the fire,
Watching the telly too.
You jump to your snowman smiling with glee,
Then you were sliding down the hill,
Like an avalanche swirling, whirling and twirling.
So make a wish,
Then fill your dish,
If there's a storm,
Definitely keep warm,
It's almost dawn,
And you have a big yawn!

Che-Hien Man (8)
Hackleton Primary School

Wintertime

When snow falls it becomes cold
When you walk outside it's bold
When it's winter the trees grow bare
The wind blows strongly, it blows your hair
Children play and make snowmen
Then they go off and see their friend Ben
Snow falls on Christmas Day
And Santa Claus is on his way.

Tom Charteress
Hackleton Primary School

In My Box

(Based on 'Magic Box' by Kit Wright)

In my box I will put a newborn baby
The sun shining on a dew-dropped grass
Snow before it's gone muddy and slushy
A couple's first kiss on a beach on an island

In my box I will put a curled up kitten
A puppy chasing its tail
The brightest star
The most colourful rainbow

In my box I will put a happy family on holiday
The winter's frost mixed with
Summer's breeze
A mother singing a lullaby to a sleeping child

In my box I will put sparkling seashells
A foamy bath being shared by twins
A birthday party when the presents are opened
A bird singing at the top of its voice

In my box I will put a snug four poster
A large poem and story book
A film without an ending
An aeroplane starting up

That's what I will put in my box.

Becky Woolley (9)
Hackleton Primary School

Football Crazy

Football is the best,
I love it, I love it,
It's the best game in the world.

The striker scores, the crowds go mad,
The goalie sulks, the team feels bad,
It's just a game,
Will we win next time?

Nathan Quinn (8)
Hackleton Primary School

Seasons

Spring
Spring is when the flowers come,
Other plants too,
Lambs are jumping up and down,
Born by the cosy ewe.

Summer
Summer is when children play,
Mostly on the beaches all day,
Children splashing in the sea,
Making sandcastles shouting, 'Yippee.'

Autumn
Autumn is when leaves fall off,
Swaying from side to side,
Sometimes like a rocket ride.

Winter
Wintertime is when it snows,
When it's very windy, fast wind blows,
People always throwing snowballs,
Ending up with really no balls.

Milly Bell (7)
Hackleton Primary School

Wind

Wind big and strong
Wind makes knees cold
It blows down trees,
Lamp posts and tents
It blows cash away
Especially on a windy day
It rips the string off kites
And blows over a bin.

Michael Coker (8)
Hackleton Primary School

Battle Of The Veggies

Yucky old veggies
Make you want to be sick
You wouldn't even want to take a tiny little lick
The sprouts come up and say, 'I'm the tastiest of them all.'
Then cabbage says, 'Be quiet! I'm trying to play pool!'
The beans interrupt, 'You don't know what you're doing.'
The carrots agree, 'We're going to start booing.'
'What?' says the pea. 'I'm a lot tastier than all you lot.'
'You're kidding,' say the cabbages. 'You all taste of snot.
Let's have a fight, apart from the sprouts.'
It lasted 10 minutes and nearly all were knocked out.
The sprouts say to the winner, 'It was just pot luck.'
A boy comes along and says, 'Don't worry - you *all* taste yuck!'

James Hutchinson (7)
Hackleton Primary School

Autumn Poem

Autumn leaves falling
Autumn leaves fall from trees
Autumn leaves turn red, yellow, brown and golden
Conkers are shiny and squirrels eat acorns
When you walk on them they make a crunchy sound
Leaves are wrinkly and crispy and dry
And they curve in the sky
They whirl, swirl, twirl
Leaves boogie and go.

Joe Niblett (7)
Hackleton Primary School

Autumn Poem

Leaves are falling off the trees,
Floating, whirling, rustling and swerving,
Leaves are turning and swirling to the ground,
In summer the leaves are green,
In autumn they are red or brown.

Conkers are shiny and brown,
Waiting on the ground,
When conkers break out of their spiky shells,
Sometimes you collect conkers when they fall off the trees,
If you battle with them I wonder who wins.

Long, fluffy tailed squirrels eat all kinds of nuts,
Squirrels snuffle along the ground looking for autumn food.

Elliot Roberts (7)
Hackleton Primary School

Autumn Poem

When it is autumn the leaves start falling
They start to go brown
There are leaves everywhere
Yellow leaves, orange leaves, brown leaves, red leaves
Everywhere are leaves

Squirrels rustling in the leaves
Children rustling in the leaves

Conkers are falling
People find them
They keep going
People have got too many.

Alfie Henman (8)
Hackleton Primary School

Wintertime

In the morning
Leaves are falling
When I call for my mates
Now no leaves are on the trees
All we see are the branches
Wobbling up and down
On the way back from my mates
Now the leaves are dropping on my head.

Charlotte Robb (7)
Hackleton Primary School

My Best Friend

My best friend is very kind
Sometimes I am rude and leave her behind
My best friend is very funny and she acts like a bunny
She has shiny and silky hair
And she's as sweet as a rose
I brought my best friend something that glows
My best friend likes May
That's the poem for the rest of the day.

Bethany Kingdom (8)
Hackleton Primary School

Wintertime

Snow, snow on the trees
Go and see what's on the floor.
Footprints in the snow,
Throwing snowballs all day.
Building snowballs,
Coal in hot fires,
Fire is very hot,
Very hot indeed.

Ben Gifford (7)
Hackleton Primary School

Wintertime

It's winter, the time when snow is falling from the sky
The snow is crunchy and the trees are bare.
The snow is falling, swirling.
The wind is whirling, howling.
Flowers dying, snow is flying.
Hedgehogs hibernating and children shivering.
Children have snowball fights.
They don't last very long because all the days are short.
Snowmen built by all the merry children.
On the 25th day of December children open their presents.
They all are merry having Christmas lunch.
Winter is the time to be young.
Winter is a fun time for playing with your toys.
If you are naughty you will get coal!

Matthew Taylor (8)
Hackleton Primary School

Autumn Poem

The leaves are falling and are flowing through the air
The leaves fall off the trees
They twirl
Orange and golden-yellow
A big bundle of leaves on the ground
People jumped in and found acorns
A squirrel came and took the acorns
To hide in its nest
Conkers shiny in their shell
Beware - shells are prickly
Conkers inside - play games
Watch your conkers don't smash!

Aaron Harrison (8)
Hackleton Primary School

Horses

Horses come in different colours,
Brown, black or white,
Sometimes they go to sleep,
And stand up all night.

Horses have different names,
Amber, Socks or Molly,
Horses are calm with dogs no matter what the type,
It could be a Dalmatian or a Collie.

Horses come in different types,
Like Shetland or Shire,
Some are small,
And grow higher and higher.

Chloe Parmenter (8)
Hackleton Primary School

Autumn Poem

The autumn leaves are falling down and falling like helicopter seeds,
They end up in big piles of green, red and brown.

The squirrels bury their nuts,
Sometimes forget where they buried them,
Sometimes they have a go at conkers.

The conkers are good for conker battles,
They can be hard conkers,
Sometimes they can be weak conkers,
Then they can be normal conkers.

David Foulger (8)
Hackleton Primary School

Wintertime

Wintertime is here again,
Waiting for the children to come out and play.
When children play in the snow,
I like to hear their footprints crunching in and out.
Snow is white and looks so clean,
I love winter, I love it when it snows.
I like to build a snowman,
I get a carrot for his nose and
Mushrooms for his eyes,
Lots of stones for his mouth,
His mouth has a smile.
I hope he never melts by the hot winter sun.
I wish winter would never go.

Hope Jarvis (8)
Hackleton Primary School

Spring Poem

Spring is a lovely time
Where creatures crawl around
Playing with their families
And dancing all around.
Creatures climbing up the trees
Saying hello to their friends,
Bees buzzing on the plants
With their mum and dad
Sisters and brothers playing on the slide
And playing with a ball and having fun!

Paige Edwards (7)
Hackleton Primary School

Washing Up Duty

Friday is my turn
To do the washing up
The plates and knives and forks
My special stripy cup
But sometimes there are things
That lurk amongst the dishes
Mouldy blue balls of fluff
That smell like rotten fishes.

A strange purple substance
A shiny, woolly thing
Some of my sister's auburn locks
A strand of furry string
A toenail of my brother's
A dead spider too
Smelly cabbage on the plates
Cutlery covered in goo.

I go to get my sister
Who's reading in her room
'Help with the washing up' I say
Like pigs will fly to the moon
As usual I was right
She utterly refused
But budged when I thumped
And hit her with my shoes.

We go down to the kitchen
To look at all the mess
My sister shrieked despite herself
And liked me even less.

Crash!
Whoops . . .

Florrie Hutchinson (11)
Hackleton Primary School

Clothes On The Washing Line

On windy days
Mum continuously puts the washing on the wooden line,
I think it's extremely boring to watch,
as she carelessly hangs Dad's shirt
upside down
and his disgracefully mucky sleeves are
dripping noisily like him drinking beer.
Mum's smart, tidy suits always appear as if they're
rushing wildly like she does at work.
Craig's warm, cosy pyjamas always look
like they're furiously moulting all over the stone patio.
Iain's short, radiant trousers are always
slowly fading to walk as if they're getting dry,
but then I see my brand new clothes
hanging on the dull line;
my small favourite jumper
with hearts on the shoulders,
my skirt
with transparent frills,
my grey slippers
that were supposed to be white.
It's like seeing bits of me
hanging there lazily on the breezy washing line.
I just can't help feeling so miserable that I'm going to be sick
and that I'm watching parts of me waving me to join them.

Natalie Litchfield (10)
Hartwell CE Primary School

Clothes In The Tumble-Dryer

On Wednesday mornings
Mum puts the waterlogged washing
In the tumble-dryer.
I think it is fun to see:
My mum's threadbare tops
Doing fantastic and amazing somersaults in one turn.
I think it is weird yet wonderful
How my dad's scrunched tops
Get blown by the clank of the old metal cylinder
Like a giant express train thundering past.
His trousers are kicking violently and powerfully
Like he is playing an anxious game of football,
My dad's rotten socks look like he is frantically throwing them away
But they keep coming back.
But when I see my clothes in the tumble-dryer, I get a freezing shiver.
It's like a part of me that's waving and saying, 'Come, come.'
My top's moving like it's playing football,
My trousers are kicking violently and playing
Against my dad's trousers,
But when the dryer stops, the trousers stop playing
And the tops stop moving
And the socks fall to the bottom of the cylinder.
Wednesday, I can't wait till next week.

Ben Simons (10)
Hartwell CE Primary School

Clothes In The Tumble-Dryer

On a rainy day,
Mum elegantly puts the washing into the tumble-dryer,
It's amusing to watch,
When the game starts,
Dad's old, dismantled shirt is spinning practically out of control
While Mum's stainless patched jeans scramble to the door,
My socks furiously fighting to get out.
On a rainy day.

Tom Barnell (10)
Hartwell CE Primary School

Clothes In The Washing Machine

On Sundays,
It's always raining hard.
Mum puts the washing in the washing machine.
I think it is exciting to watch how she puts them in.
It looks like everyone is swimming,
Trying to swim, faster and faster,
Trying to push through,
Coming first at the finish line,
Be a champion!
My brother's look like they are going to
Do a twirling somersault,
Having fun in the dark blue water,
Instead of concentrating to win the race.
They look as if they are going to swim away.
My dad's jeans look like they are jogging
Frantically into the dark distance,
Faster and faster, quicker and quicker.
My patched jeans look like I'm horse riding
Quickly into the dark, dull distance.

Toni Oyston (11)
Hartwell CE Primary School

Clothes In The Tumble-Dryer

On dull Wednesdays,
Mum shoves the drenched and dazzling
Washing in the dryer.
It tells short stories.
Dad's tattered and threadbare overalls
Grasping the worn out van wheel in rage,
Going round and round the hypnotising roundabout.
He is pipping furiously, trying to get out
Of the traffic-jammed roundabout.
Mum's elegant and splendid trousers
Zooming down the shopping aisle as fast as she can,
Trying to get the last Christmas turkey.
A bloodied-up T-shirt of Dan's,
In a horrific fight of doom.
Sarah's dazzling hipsters,
Bobbing up and down in a mad crowd of people,
Singing away at Home Grown's concert.
Then there's me.
I'm not sure I like watching it,
It's like parts of my life slipping away.

Amy Lewis (11)
Hartwell CE Primary School

Clothes In The Washing Machine

I shivered
As I watched
My brother's radiant shirt
Forcibly and frantically
Fight his way to the front.
And saw my mum's
Sophisticated trousers
Appear as if they were jogging
Through the deserted, lush, green grass.
Then I spotted my streamlined
Swimming costume
Competitively
Fly past
The other losing swimmers.
And then,
I vigorously laughed
When I saw
My embarrassing dad's
Hideous trainers
Clumsily stumble over the barking dog.
I shivered as I watched
The clothes in the washing machine.

Danielle Georgia Pike (10)
Hartwell CE Primary School

Clothes In The Airing Cupboard

On typical days
Mum gently places the clothes in the boiling airing cupboard;
I think it's baking inside
As she softly hangs Dad's threadbare jeans
Faded and crumpled
They carefully wave, like he's driving down the road.
Mum's large variety of extensive coats, gracefully walking me
to school.

Tara's patterned pants covered with radiant stars,
Twinkling and shimmering
Which appear as if she's running in the active playground,
Legs imaginatively attached.
But when I briskly glance at my favourite clothes,
My snazzy jeans
With patches on the knees,
My groovy T-shirt
With the words 'Love and Peace' elegantly written,
It seems like parts of me are falling apart.
I can't help feeling I'm not my usual self,
Walking and talking
And I'm gracefully watching;
Seeing parts of me . . .
Frantically waving me to join them.

Siobhan Burditt (10)
Hartwell CE Primary School

Clothes In A Cupboard

On Friday mornings,
when Mum puts the warm ironing in the cupboard,
as she neatly hangs Dad's shirt
on the long orange pole,
as he lazily puts a puzzle together,
carefully reaching down to pick up a piece
from the cold, hard floor.
Mum's trousers standing still
as she anxiously waits in line
to buy an expensive new dress.
My brother's red and white rugby shirt,
steadily waiting for the game to start.
My sister's sparkly skirt,
waiting carelessly in the long line to get into a cool new nightclub,
and my clothes;
my favourite white jeans and hilarious Spongebob top,
standing playing daring and adventurous twenty-one dares
with all my friends,
Sian, Siobhan, Danielle, Cerys and Jessica,
laughing loudly as timid Cerys
gets picked to do a humiliating dare,
although,
I can't help feeling I'm missing something,
something big,
I just don't know what.

Bethan Amy Halder (10)
Hartwell CE Primary School

Spinning Clothes In The Tumble-Dryer

During the misty evening,
Mum curiously chucks the filthy washing
in the miniature tumble-dryer.
I continuously glance at Dad's radiant shirt;
it frantically spins out of control every now and then.
Mum's denim jeans rapidly jog backwards.
Sabia's
glinting leotard
flexibly bends; it steadily taps the
top of the whirling and hurling tumble-dryer.
It suddenly performs
energetic somersaults
twirling round and round
but mine swiftly yet calmly
just float.
It's weird watching
my silky top elegantly dart about.
It's weird watching it
drift.

Sian Egan (10)
Hartwell CE Primary School

Ironing Board

I watch the elegant clothes
Immediately stretch side to side
As if they're anxiously praying for help,
The blaze of the flame,
They twitch and suffer.
Nothing can stop them escaping.
The sound of the furious steam
Will make them feel extremely flat and weak,
The pressure is on.
I continue watching the elegant clothes
Move backward and forwards.

Jade Curtis (11)
Hartwell CE Primary School

Clothes In The Cupboard

On average days
I look in the aged and stale cupboard,
The clothes seem to humanly move,
I think I'm imagining things,
Sometimes I don't.
I can't help but notice
And see
My dad's black and threadbare top sleeve
Move toughly as if it has a dirty wrench in his hand,
Moving it slowly as if it's getting tighter.
My mum's blue flowered dress sleeve
In a ladylike position elegantly
Holding a glass of wine in her hand.
I hear the clanging of the glasses.

Luke Gambrill (11)
Hartwell CE Primary School

Clothes In The Washing Machine

On bleak winter days when I'm stuck inside,
I watch the clothes in the washing machine.
They spin and tumble continuously as if they're alive:
My mum's ragged fleece spins furiously like on a mouse wheel,
Mine and my sister's shirts scramble vulnerably to get out,
My dad's worn out trousers fight the other clothes
trying to break loose,
All the socks punch and fight aggressively
at the window, trying to get free.
Sometimes I get scared that the washed clothes are going to get out.
I like watching the clothes go round
on the bleak winter days of the year.

David Knott (11)
Hartwell CE Primary School

The Washing Line

On sunny but blowy days
Mum always hangs the washing on the line;
I find it funny when I watch
As Mum hangs Dad's many coloured and coffee-stained shirts
Upside down,
It flaps its arms in confusion and dismay.
Mum's radiant patterned jeans crazily blow
Continuously out of
Control.
But when Mum hangs up my clothes:
My ragged blue Chelsea FC top which is blowing frantically
As if it is desperately running for the goal,
And my thread-ridden cargo trousers
Which hang on the line.
But I still find it funny on
Sunny but blowy
Days.

Harry Wright (11)
Hartwell CE Primary School

Clothes In The Wardrobe

As my mum puts the
delicate clothes in the pine wardrobe,
I sit and glare at them.
My mum's sophisticated, fiery jackets
march along the rail.
My dad's patchy trousers
paddle in a gentle way.
It's kind of funny,
my brother's clanky shirts
look as if they're playing.
My elegant jodhpurs
look as if they're riding
through the breezy winds.

Nikita Pedro (11)
Hartwell CE Primary School

Clothes On The Clothes Horse

Every day my frustrated mum would carefully
Place the soggy clothes on the rusty clothes horse, and
Every day I used to watch them dry.
Today is no different.
I am sitting on the old and faded sofa with a bag of sweets,
Watching them dry.
It is always fun to watch.
Dad's old and ragged T-shirt always seems as if it is lazily lounging,
Watching television, roasting in front of the blazing fire.
Weird really,
That's what Dad usually does.
Mum's warm and radiant jumper appears as if it is frantically dusting
The almighty fireplace as she does every week.
Poor Mum,
She has so much to do in such a little time.
My baby sister's tiny and bright suit, on the bottom pole,
Looks as if she is hurrying along the threadbare carpet.
Finally my favourite warm and bulky fleece
Standing stiffly in front of the television,
There is a shiver down my spine when I am not wearing my fleece.
Maybe it's just me.

Sophia Jarvis (10)
Hartwell CE Primary School

Clothes In The Washing Machine

On dark, dingy days,
Mum carelessly shoves the washing
into the washing machine.
It's fun to watch,
her sophisticated top
remarkably swim to the front,
then get tragically overtaken by
Dad's radiant shirt controlling the car,
wildly and madly spinning out of control.
Peter's potato-like socks on stage now,
amazingly doing what looks like a double act
with another mouldy twin,
ending with an extraordinary row of complicated loops.
Mike's jumper
vigorously doing dangerous diving into the hot water,
a magician facing his own life.
Chris' shorts,
having a risky stroll
by the darkly lit ponds, frantically dashing on,
That's what I see on dark, dingy days.

Bethany Dixon (10)
Hartwell CE Primary School

Clothes In The Washing Machine

On Sundays
Mum puts the radiant clothes in the unfortunate washing machine,
I think it's actually boring to watch
as she throws Dad's signed shirt and smart black trousers in,
mixed with other clothes.
His shirt somersaults acrobatically and his trousers jog violently
in a circle.
Mum's long flowered skirt dancing in a circle,
her top exercising frantically through and through until they clash.
Lee's blue jeans running,
his baggy shirt shouting.
Chris' motorbike outfit on a motorbike circling in and out.
My flared jeans resting, my football top (Brazil) cheering.
On Sundays
Mum puts the washing in the washing machine.

Laura Chapman (11)
Hartwell CE Primary School

The Ironing Pile

The smell of ash burning continuously,
and the look of old and creased clothes,
My lazy mum was ironing again.
The patched sleeves hanging off the enormous ironing board edge
made it look like it screamed tremendously.
Dad's shirts are ripped like a mammoth chainsaw
and burnt with an iron.
My sister's freaky, threadbare shirts
were full of soggy tissues and rusty chains.
My shirts are football mad, scruffy and worn out,
trying to catch a ball, but I've lost a part of me.

Hayden Carnegie (10)
Hartwell CE Primary School

Clothes In The Washing Machine

My brother's dull
T-shirts in the washing
machine on a normal
washing day are
somersaulting in an
elegant way.
His other enthusiastic
jumping T-shirts are
frayed from pinching
and punching each other.
My mum's incredible
twisty shirts are
trying to force their
way out with their
furious arms.
Her other twinkling shirts
are raving mad
trying to strangle each other.

Carrie-Anne Kitchen (10)
Hartwell CE Primary School

Clothes In The Tumble-Dryer

On normal Saturdays, Mum puts the clothes in the tumble-dryer.
Dad's old ragged T-shirt is continuously forcing its way out.
The furious heat is too much for Dad's T-shirt.
Mum's T-shirt is rolling madly down the slithery hill as if it is in a race.
My trousers are going round as if they are doing front flips madly.
My T-shirt is slapping frantically at all the other clothes.

Declan Warner (11)
Hartwell CE Primary School

Clothes On The Washing Line

On blustery cold days
My mum always hangs out the old, tatty washing,
Which always comes out with unknown movements.
It's fun to watch my brand new spanking clothes
Jump about frantically as if we have just won the rugby World Cup.
And my dad's new, shining clothes are waving frantically,
As if West Bromwich Albion scored the first goal ever in the match.
And my mum's shining clothes look as if
They are trying to reach for something, like an iron,
Yet they are just barely hanging on to the twelve-year-old washing line,
At the mercy of every piece of stray wind imaginable
Which is coming and stopping.
But my clothes are continuously separating from each other,
And they're badly separating from each other and from me.
I can almost hear them calling me over.

Jarred Webb (11)
Hartwell CE Primary School

Clothes In The Tumble-Dryer

My brother's awkward clothes turn and twist,
Forcing their way through,
Bashing and slapping each other.
Shirts ferociously attack and flatten.
They moan, mumble and grumble.
The somersault and roll.
They even elbow each other.
And all of this is just to prove a point.
My father's jeans kick and run round and round as they go,
They never stop until they stumble and fall.
Mum's dresses move softly and carefully, taking their time,
And my white school shirt panicking all the time.
Now it's stopped so I can put on my extra part of me.

Jordan Dickson (10)
Hartwell CE Primary School

Clothes On The Washing Line

On breezy days,
Mum hangs the washing on the old, green line.
I think it is interesting to watch
As she pegs up my unused football sweater
The arms appear to be frantically running
As if I'm running with the powerful ball, ready to kick it into the goal.
Mum's humorous T-shirt looks as if the arms
Are carefully opening and closing the ancient metallic oven,
and taking delicious food out.
Then Dad's denim jacket's arms,
They look as if they're cautiously driving a bulky lorry,
Delivering goods to gloomy and deserted places and factories.
Also, Lorraine's sophisticated trousers,
They seem as if they're gradually jogging towards the chocolate shop.
Zoe's radiant coats look as if they're frantically dancing
All night long, boogieing to the beat.
Christopher's grey socks, which are supposed to be white
Just look as if they're viciously running away from
the bouncing balloons.
Ryan's threadbare vest which isn't meant to be elasticated
Looks as if it's spinning rapidly around.
But when I see my favourite Good Charlotte top
Flapping around in the gentle breeze,
It feels that I'm watching part of me,
Waving at me to join them
With all the excitement and fun.

Lucy Drake (11)
Hartwell CE Primary School

Streets Of London

Dirty, dirty,
Bare-footed and poorly,
Orphans beg for a crust of bread,
All in vain with a broken leg,
All on the streets of London.
Horses and carriages roam on by
Causing pollution on busy streets.
By day there's rats, by night there's bats,
All on the streets of London.
Deadly diseases fill the air,
See people dancing with a great bear,
Scruffy boys, scruffy girls,
Only rags can be seen,
Not a shilling, not a penny, no brass farthings to be seen.
All on the streets of London.

Thomas Shaw (11)
Park Junior School

The Boy Child

Sitting on the street all day,
without a penny to display.
Loathing for a crust of bread
and something to rest their sleepy head.

Ladies and gentlemen passing by,
pretending not to hear them cry.
Sniggering and laughing at their joy,
at seeing a poor and little boy.

Feeling weak at the seam,
having a bed would be his dream.
All the sights of the shops are plain,
as he sits in the pouring rain.

Meltressa Smith (11) & Michaela Parmar (10)
Park Junior School

Gleaming, Sparkling Christmas Lights

Gleaming, sparkling Christmas lights
flicker on the Christmas tree.
Diamonds and stones of many kinds,
night by night
the lights flicker by.
Gleaming
in the midnight air
dots appear everywhere,
red, blue, yellow
and bright white
lights appear, making
silver, gold and purple.
And many sparkle,
in the air you feel it,
coming above your head, sparkling
Christmas lights
are all you want.

Loreen Wong (11)
Park Junior School

Christmas Is Coming

When Christmas is here it's
glossy, glittery, glorious, sparkling
icicles, shine beautifully, stand
out, fabulous, exotic snowmen.
Magical, see-through, sweet
frosted snow,
    slushy,
        salty,
            watery.
Oh! It's gone.

Priya Patel (10)
Park Junior School

School Likes And Dislikes

I like
Ace art
Challenging chess club
Terrific teachers
Miraculous maths
Ingenious ICT
Super snacks
Perfect playtimes
Lovely lunches
Tremendous trumpet lessons
Resourceful reading
Creative cooking
Splendid singing
Marvellous merits
Fantastic friends
Luminous literacy
Magnificent music
Grand geography
Hairy history
And
Awe-inspiring head teacher's awards.
I dislike
Sorrowful strikes.

Connor Baird (9)
Park Junior School

The Frog

The frog jumped in a hole,
And saw an angry mole.
The frog leapt up the tree
And met a buzzing bee.
The frog swam in the lake
And got bitten by a snake.
He went back to his log,
The sad and lonely frog.

Frances Dickson (8)
Pattishall CE Primary School

My Poem

Roses are red
And violets blue
I love my daddy
And he loves me too

Mummies are gentle
And mummies are kind
I think my mummy's
The best I could find

Brothers are naughty
And brothers are mad
If I'd no brother
Then I would be sad

I love my family
My family loves me
They always make me
As happy as can be.

Jenny Hill (7)
Pattishall CE Primary School

Miss Smartypants

Miss Smartypants thinks she's the best,
But really she's no better than the rest.
Every playtime she chats up the boys,
And she thinks she has all the best toys.
One day Miss Smartypants was boasting loudly,
Swishing her hair from side to side proudly,
When Mr Holiday (our teacher) crept up behind her,
Making Miss Smartypants turn and gasp, 'Oh sir!'
'You child!' he shouted. 'Was that you I could hear from the hall?'
She felt embarrassed and really small.
'Yes, Mr Holiday,' she cried in shame,
And after that day she was never the same.

Charlie Taylor (8)
Pattishall CE Primary School

Lanzarote

When we went to Lanzarote
We saw parrots doing funny tricks,
Riding a bicycle and talking to us
And all different things.

We went to the beach
And played in the sand.
Every night we went out to the bar,
We ate lots of pizza.

We met a boy called Lewis.
On his last day it was his eighth birthday,
We gave him the rock I found
On the beach.

Then Mummy wrote on it in nail varnish
And we gave it to Lewis
Before he went home.

We played in the pool all day long
And on the last day,
We went to see the aeroplane fly off.

Amber Mortimer (7)
Pattishall CE Primary School

Moonlight

From faraway land
I cast my spell
By my bedside
I can see my aunt standing by the light
Oh little moon, you shine so bright
My heart in the light
Brother light
Oh Sister bright
You are my life
Oh Mother sight
Oh Father might
Show yourself
Your light will melt
When suddenly it glitters like the sun
Oh Brother light
Oh Sister bright
Oh Mother sight
Oh Father might
Do you want to see my lovely sight?

Betty Sweet (8)
Pattishall CE Primary School

Ellie And The Jelly

There once was a girl called Ellie,
All she ever ate was jelly,
Her tummy went wobberly
And her jumper went bobberly,
Now all she ever does is watch telly.

Jenny Dunn (9)
Rockingham Primary School

The Boy From Spain

There once was a boy from Spain,
He was in such a lot of pain,
He began to throb,
Then started to sob,
Which eventually drove him insane.

Nathan Ward (9)
Rockingham Primary School

A Girl Called Stace

There once was a girl called Stace
She always came last in the race,
When she walked down the street
With her very ugly feet
And also a horrible face.

Danny Bloomfield (9)
Rockingham Primary School

Flowers - Haiku

Flowers they are bright
Together they sway all day.
They dance in the breeze.

Bethan Watson (8)
Rockingham Primary School

The Big Tree - Haiku

The tree in the woods
is so big that I cannot
climb it anymore.

Tom Stone (9)
Rockingham Primary School

Infant Nativity

I n the hall
N oisy children
F ingering costumes
A ngry music
N aughty sheep
T all shepherds

N aughty stars
A ngels
T alking children
I rritating noise
V ery good children
I nfant play
T insel
Y ellow stars.

Kayley Smith (9)
Rockingham Primary School

Elephants - Haiku

I drink my water
through my trunk, that is how I
can drink my water.

Jake McGinlay (9)
Rockingham Primary School

The Flowers - Haiku

The flowers are so
Beautiful, roses are red
My top favourite.

Carl Smith (9)
Rockingham Primary School

Tree - Haiku

The tree is tall, it
Blows gently in the wind, it
Has twenty branches.

Sarah Gould (9)
Rockingham Primary School

Roses - Haiku

Roses are pretty
And so the bees come to rest
To take the pollen.

Harriet Truss (9)
Rockingham Primary School

Boredom - Haiku

I lie on my bed
Watching TV and staring
Out of the window.

Ellie Tait (9)
Rockingham Primary School

Flowers - Haiku

They smell very nice
In every garden they look
Sweet, they smell so sweet.

Lyndsey McCormick (8)
Rockingham Primary School

Infant Nativity

I n the hall
N oisy children
F abulous costumes
A ngels
N aughty innkeeper
T atty shepherds

N oisy children
A bsolutely brilliant
T hree kings
I ncredible
V isitors to Jesus
I nfants are great
T errible, no way
Y oung performers.

Jack Brown (8)
Rockingham Primary School

Infant Nativity

I n the hall
N oisy children
F ingering costumes
A ngry shepherds
N ervous children
T iny Mason tripped over the bench

N erve-racking play
A nnoying, sleepy shepherd
T remendous potential
I rritating noises
V oices are loud
I nvited guests
T ickling costumes
Y ellow crowns.

Amylouise Lines (9)
Rockingham Primary School

Summertime - Haiku

In the summer I
Plant some seeds and water and
Feed them more and more.

James Pender (8)
Rockingham Primary School

Bears

Bears, bears are everywhere.
Some are black, some are brown,
Some even have a frown.
Some are scary,
Some are friendly,
Some don't even care.
Some are real,
Some are fake,
Sadly some are dead.

Conor Duncan (8)
St Patrick's Catholic Primary School, Corby

Chess

I play chess with my cheetah.
My cheetah's name is Jim.
He has been known to beat me,
But mostly I beat him.
Yesterday I was defeated,
That's because my cheetah cheated!

Aidan Black (7)
St Patrick's Catholic Primary School, Corby

On Hallowe'en

Flames as bright as orange
Pumpkins glowing in the sky.
Glowing yellow lights
Flickering in the night.
Fat orange pumpkins
Glowing in the night.
Children looking out of windows
Getting a fright.
Hanging skeletons people see,
Making children scream.
People with masks and cloaks,
Knocking on doors, asking for
Sweets and more and more.

Paige Broughton (9)
St Patrick's Catholic Primary School, Corby

Midnight Wanders

As the sky gleams,
The sky is dark blue,
Stars twinkle and fly,
Wind races through the trees
With a herd of bees.
As it gets darker,
The sky gets as dull as an old gravestone,
Rain shoots down as lightning flashes
And thunder roars,
Then the moon starts fading in the
Pitch-black clouds.

Kayleigh Carlton (9)
St Patrick's Catholic Primary School, Corby

The Music I Like

The music I like
May very well shock,
Don't give me boy bands,
Hit me with rock!

When I listen to Metallica,
I think of pain,
They drive me crazy,
They drive me insane!

Then bands like Chilli Peppers,
They are so cool,
When they are on stage,
They ain't nobody's fool!

Nirvana were tops,
With Kurt at the mic,
They formed into Foos -
The music I like!

Ciarán McLaughlin (10)
St Patrick's Catholic Primary School, Corby

Ice Lolly

Red rocket, white rocket
Both on a stick,
Lick, lick, lick,
My tongue shines like a brick.
Do not stop 'til the red rocket melts
Into the ground
Never to be found,
Red rocket, white rocket
Both on a stick.

Robyn McGilly (8)
St Patrick's Catholic Primary School, Corby

My Favourite Colour

My favourite colour is blue -
Or is it purple?
In fact I think it's green
For a turtle.

My favourite colour is red -
Or is it pine,
The colour of my bed?

My favourite colour is white -
Or is it star bright?

I think my favourite colour is brown -
The colour of my eyes.

But I don't know,
I've still got time to decide,
Because in my mind
A colour doesn't fade or die.

Leah Brown (9)
St Patrick's Catholic Primary School, Corby

Wonderland Of Rainbows And Rain

The sun burning over everyone,
The rain comes,
Drip-drop, drip-drop.
The sun shines like a golden eagle.
Out comes a rainbow with all its golden colours,
It is like a colourful bridge
As it shines like an angel.
Now the rainbow's disappearing,
The colours are fading,
The sun comes back out through the golden rain.

Brogan Carlton (7)
St Patrick's Catholic Primary School, Corby

Oscar

He has big brown eyes,
A nice wet nose,
Pointed ears,
And he likes to pose.

He has hairy feet,
A tail that wags,
Nice strong teeth,
And he likes to play tag.

He goes out in the garden
And chases the birds,
Has lots of fun
And always comes third.

He is such a cutie,
We all love him so,
Our dog Oscar,
Has a long way to go!

Abby Smith (11)
St Patrick's Catholic Primary School, Corby

Water, Water

Water, water everywhere,
Water, water in my hair,
Water, water that I share,
Water, water, we must care.
Drip, drop, out comes the mop,
Drip, drop, pick up a top,
Drip, drop, as I hop,
Drip, drop, as I stop.
Drip, drop, I can have a lollipop!

Brogan Connor (9)
St Patrick's Catholic Primary School, Corby

While . . .

While children are fast asleep
Mice peep and squeak.
While children are busy playing
Trees are swaying and waving.
While children are eating breakfast
Bats are having a rest.
While children are having their dinner
Whales are growing thinner.

Danielle Curtis (9)
St Patrick's Catholic Primary School, Corby

Hallowe'en Sights

One Hallowe'en we saw
A silver moon across the sky,
Big and fat pumpkins
Sitting in a row.
Cats' eyes shining like metal,
Witches with their broomsticks
And sparkling nails.

Sammy-Jo Brooks (8)
St Patrick's Catholic Primary School, Corby

Splish, Splash, Splosh

Splish, splash, splosh, goes the water when I swim.
Splish, splash, splosh, goes the water in the tub.
Gulp, gulp, gulp, goes the water when I drink.
Drip, drip, drip, goes the water from the tap.
Drop, drop, drop, goes the water when it rains.
I hear water when it goes splish, splash, splosh.

Esther Abe (10)
St Patrick's Catholic Primary School, Corby

What Is White?

What is white? Snow is white
Blowing gently and light.
What is green? The grass is green
With pretty flowers in-between.
What is blue? The sky is blue
With clouds that look like cows going 'moo'.
What is red? A rose is red
But now it needs to go to bed.
What is yellow? The sun is yellow
With loads of people in the sun who bellow.
What is black? A cat is black
In the night while having a nap.
What is grey? A rabbit is grey
If you go near it, it will just hop away.
What is brown? Chocolate is brown,
When people don't get chocolate they all start to frown.
What is pink? Raspberries are pink,
When people eat them they always wink.
What is gold? Gold is gold,
When people get gold it makes their hands get cold.
What is peach? A peach is peach,
Just a peach.

Bethanie Donaldson (9)
St Patrick's Catholic Primary School, Corby

A Crispy Cold Night

The sky is dark blue
Filled with stars so bright;
A little bird just flew
To where the moon shines light,
Looking down on the street
To see the snow so white:
He saw a wriggly worm to eat -
So flew down from the night.

Kharla Hassan (10)
St Patrick's Catholic Primary School, Corby

A Day In The Life Of Dolton Calderwood

Each and every morning
I always wake up yawning
As I get myself out of bed
And rub my weary head
Off to the bathroom I go
To wash and brush my teeth I know.

Then it's downstairs for some Ready Brek
Mum shouting, 'Hurry up, or I'll break your neck,'
When I'm all done and slip on my shoes,
Mum is too busy watching the news.

As we head off to school it's a bit of a hurry
With Mum doing sixty and saying, 'Don't worry,
We will get to school in one piece.'
Mum shouts to me, 'Get on your fleece.'

When I get into school and head to my class
It feels like the morning has been a mad dash
With my teacher saying, 'Good afternoon.'
Mr Latimer is being sarcastic I assume.

The day comes to an end at three-fifteen,
My dad in the car park is nowhere to be seen.
He'll be zooming down Patrick Road,
Doesn't he know the Highway Code?

When I get home and have my tea
My loving family always do see,
Not forgetting my big dog Winston,
He's always there to have some fun.

Off to bed then I must go,
Ready to start again tomorrow.

Dolton Calderwood (11)
St Patrick's Catholic Primary School, Corby

My Rabbit

I had a rabbit called Mellow,
He was buttercup-yellow.
He liked lying in the sun and always had fun.
He ran on the lawn
And got pricked by the thorns.
Mellow chased the neighbour's cat.
He was very fat.
I've got pictures of him in a grass skirt,
One's of him covered in dirt.
Pictures of him dressed up as a clown,
One's of him wearing a crown.
So that's what I know about my rabbit,
And as you see, he has strange habits.

Shannon Carey (9)
St Patrick's Catholic Primary School, Corby

Football

Liverpool, Man U, Celtic and Rangers,
All take part in football favours.
They are always in the goal,
Caring about a human soul.

1, 2, 3 or 4,
We want goals galore.
Dribbling, passing, shooting stars,
They can kick the ball to Mars.
Red, green, blue or black,
Everyone gets a pat on the back!

Molly Chisholm (10)
St Patrick's Catholic Primary School, Corby

Windy Mornings

Waking up by the chattering window
Above my sleepy head,
No, I won't get up out of my pyjamas or bed,
Stomping down the massive stairs,
Hairs standing up on my back,
Warm cornflakes there,
But I can't bear that horrible, terrible wind!

Treading over the icy road, cars, buses and vans,
Making me want to have a fire in my hands.
At last I arrive at my freezing cold school,
But oops! I have broken a rule!

Lauren Tosh (11)
St Patrick's Catholic Primary School, Corby

Motor Crossing

Racing down the muddy track
With the wind in my hair
Everyone stands, looks and stares
The wheels are turning
My belly is churning
There's mud on my face, this motor crossing is ace.
I've had a fun time
Now back to the start line
To do another lap of the track.

Gavin Smith (10)
St Patrick's Catholic Primary School, Corby

Whatever The Weather

Whilst we were walking through the woods,
My friend and I decided to put up our hoods!
Lightning struck a tree nearby,
My friend and I shrieked and cried!

We walked underneath the dark grey clouds
When rain and lightning were howling out loud!
I ran shivering and wet towards a tree,
It was safe so I shouted to my friend, 'Follow me!'

We came to a dark, big, black house,
All we could hear was lightning and a squeak from a mouse.
We came to the big black gates that gave a creak,
And the little mouse that gave a squeak!

We went inside, staring around,
And wiping our muddy feet on the dirty ground!
We saw some spiders on the floor,
They were heading for the opened front door!

This had gone terribly wrong!
'But as long as we stick together we'll be strong.'
But my eyes were full of dread and fear
For there was something that drew near and near.

It was just my shadow upon the wall,
It made me look scary and tall!
That's enough!
I hate this weather!

Katie Scarratt (10)
St Patrick's Catholic Primary School, Corby

One Morning

I wake up one morning with a
Window above my head.
I am so tired, I can't get out of bed.
My mum comes up the stairs with sticky-up hair,
She hands a cup over to me,
I look inside and it's tea.
I go down the stairs and put my clothes on,
Then my little sister starts singing an annoying song.
I run to school because I am late,
I am lucky I am not a Victorian,
Or they would close the gate.
The bell goes without me noticing,
I press the buzzer with a *bing!*
Oh no, I forgot, what a terrible morning,
I hope my poem's not making you yawning.

Conner Tosh (10)
St Patrick's Catholic Primary School, Corby

Colours

Colours, colours everywhere,
I don't know why they are there;
Colours in the kitchen,
Colours in the air,
Colours in the jungle
Where elephants stare;
I guess I know why colours are everywhere -
To brighten people's faces,
That's why!

Olivia Olton (9)
St Patrick's Catholic Primary School, Corby

Sudden Snow

One minute it was here,
And the next it melted away -
Just melted away.
Didn't stay for too long,
But while it was here,
Trees were covered in white,
They all looked so pretty,
With branches sparkling bright.
We all loved the snow
For the time it was here -
But now we'll have to wait
Until it snows next year.

Jamie-Leigh Connor (9)
St Patrick's Catholic Primary School, Corby

Star Light

If you place a diamond in the sky
It will almost look like a star
Even if you place it high
Or if you put it really far
It will look really bright
Shining in the dark, dark night

Star light, star bright
The diamond will keep you safe tonight
Diamonds and stars are much the same
The only difference is their name
So the next time you see a star so bright
Make a wish before you say goodnight.

Rebecca Morgan (9)
St Patrick's Catholic Primary School, Corby

Beach In A Storm

Sunshine hides,
Waves crashing,
Boats drowning,
Rotting sand.
Thunder rumbles,
Lightning strikes!
Smelly stones.
Sky turns black,
Big waves swallow fish,
Storm rain makes windows smash,
Storm clouds come,
The beach is in a storm.

Sean King (7)
St Patrick's Catholic Primary School, Corby

Rushing Wind

Fierce, fiery wind, rushing to and fro.
Wind whispering in the dark.
Whistling wind blowing loudly.
The wind whistling softly,
Howling louder than ever.
A-rustling and a-scrabbling, screeched the wind.

Lucy Herring (10)
St Thomas More RC Primary School, Kettering

There Was A Young Girl Called Mare

There was a young girl called Mare
Who decided to punch Tony Blair,
He ran to his car,
The police were in the bar
And he ended up in intensive care.

Khama Langdon (10)
St Thomas More RC Primary School, Kettering

It Was So Quiet

It was so quiet that I heard
Snowflakes melt into the gravel.
It was so quiet that I heard
An ant strolling to a fruit basket.
It was so quiet that I heard
My eyelids flicker like lightning.
It was so quiet that I heard
A raindrop trickle down my back.
It was so quiet that I heard
Bubbles pop gently.
It was so quiet that I heard
A baby's heart beat softly.

Arlee Roe (10)
St Thomas More RC Primary School, Kettering

Sounds

A whisper, a whistle, says the wind.
A moaning and a puffing.
A rustle and bustle, shouts the wind,
A rattle and a roaring.
A howling and a banging, bellows the wind,
A groaning and a crashing.
A moaning and a shouting, yells the wind,
A squawk and a rattling.
A squeak and a sniffle, says the wind,
A swooshing and a swaying.
No sound, whispers the wind,
Just silence.

Emily Portch (11)
St Thomas More RC Primary School, Kettering

'Woof!' Said The Cat

'Woof!' said the cat.
'Squeak!' said the dog.
'Oink!' said the mosquito.
'Cluck!' said the hog.

'Hee-haw!' said the owl.
'Snort!' said the ant.
'Roar!' said the mice
And the pig bought some pants.

'Moo!' said the lion.
'Quack!' said the horse.
'Roof!' said the butterfly
And the crocodile got divorced.

Scott Parker (10)
St Thomas More RC Primary School, Kettering

Silence

The wind roaring, rustling one day,
Whispering, whistling, whooshing the next.
Crackling, crashing, creaking,
Squeaking, swooshing, squawking,
Silence!

Emma Giddings (11)
St Thomas More RC Primary School, Kettering

A Young Boy Who Thought He Was Flash

A young boy who thought he was flash,
Leapt into the pool with a splash,
But he was so vain,
And really a pain,
So he got out and played in the trash.

Francesca Denny (10)
St Thomas More RC Primary School, Kettering

Snow

When I woke up this morning
And glanced out of the misty window
I was unaccustomed
To the snow sprinkling lightly on the ground.

Floating down and down
Onto the dozing, drowsy town,
Freezing the still waters of the garden pond.
Hushing all the noises
And covering all the trees.

When I got out there, the snow was soft.
The dazzling whiteness gleaming and glistening.
The snow crunching under my feet.
Everything was silent.

Thomas Brown (10)
St Thomas More RC Primary School, Kettering

The Wind

The howling hurricane hardly hammered
On the gargling gate,
The whispering wind whistled wildly,
The crashing door rattled in the wind,
The flying washing wildly waved,
Ugly umbrellas unhooked themselves,
Trashing tornadoes took tractors,
Tearing them up.

Michael Newman (11)
St Thomas More RC Primary School, Kettering

Amazing Animal Alphabet

A lligators angrily eat ants and allow antelopes to annoy apes.
B eautiful butterflies bat balls with bears, while baboons
and black bunnies play ball.
C olourful cats eat cake while cute chicks cuddle with care.
D aring dragons dive down on delightful deer and dirty dogs
drop dogs on drains.
E normous elephants eat eggs and emus look envious.
F ast-food fish in frying pans for frogs.
G reat giraffes gawp at green goats eating grass.
H orrible horses hit helpless hippos with hooves.
I guanas incredibly engulf illuminous indigo snakes.
J uvenile jaguars jump on jammy Japanese jelly babies.
K icking koalas kill kick-boxing kangaroos.
L eaping lamas lick limes and lemons and leeches at lovely lynx.
M inute minnows maximise music while moles give
mallards manicures.
N aughty nits make newts nauseous by knitting nappies.
O wls eat oranges while ostriches open neutron bombs.
P olar bears prowl peacefully and pretty puppies pick pink posies.
Q uail queue and cool queens are queasy.
R egal rabbits roll down coral reefs on rollerblades.
S wans swim in the sun and skunks stink.
T igers tear toads and torture tortoises terribly.
U seless ewes use unlimited umbrellas in utility units.
V ine snakes vacuum vans and vixens vandalise vineyards.
W allabies wear wellies while wolves wail.
X -ray fish examine excellent hair extensions
Y aks yak and yodel.
Z ebras play xylophones while zooming around zoos.

Natasha Johnson (11)
St Thomas More RC Primary School, Kettering

The Wind's Journey

As I sprint across the rooftops
Laughing at flustered people down below
Toppling all the chimney tops,
Making clothes on the line flow.

Then I get to the beach
Prodding fishermen's cats from their sleep,
Watching waves crash against the shore.
Next I rush across the ocean deep.

Soon I see crabs and lobsters
And many brightly coloured fish,
Then there are the sharks,
Swimming across the sea with a haughty swish.

I see the many different countries and islands
I gaze at sea and sand,
Seeing rainforests and deserts,
In my never-ending journey across the land.

Natalie Milmoe (10)
St Thomas More RC Primary School, Kettering

The Raging Wind

The raging wind rushes, roaring down the road
The raging wind gently whistles and whispers through cracks
The raging wind howls, moans and groans past houses
The raging wind then went totally soundless.

Casey Lynch (11)
St Thomas More RC Primary School, Kettering

Snow Poem

Snow twirling, tumbling, sparkling
In the dark night sky.
Snow outside on trees
Above the narrow streets
Falling, as the trees shake
In the winter wind.
When I look out the window
I see a dazzling blaze
Of frothy cream hot chocolate carpet,
Covering everything, from bumpy grass
To the tall tower on top of the town church.
The tracks of dogs and people clearly seen.
Snowflakes of different shapes and sizes.
Cold, soft, scented snow, pure, clear and spotless,
Camouflaged rocks, roofs and railings.

Charlotte Clark (9)
St Thomas More RC Primary School, Kettering

Snow Poem

As snowflakes fall to the ground they catch the sunlight
And they glisten, sparkle and shine like stars at night,
Completely camouflaged,
Nothing in sight,
Apart from the soft, white snow.

People with their footprints ruin the effect,
They never think what they are doing.
Children making angels in the snow,
Not knowing where to go.

As I was walking through the town,
Snow kept falling down and down.

Natalie Pietrasiewicz (10)
St Thomas More RC Primary School, Kettering

Snow

It's wintertime, the snow is falling
In all different directions. The weather's appalling.
When I walk outside I can feel the crispy, crunchy sound
Underneath my feet.
The snow is nice and silky sleek.

A carpet of snow
Still and soft
Sparkling and self-scented.
No footprints to see
Except from the squirrels.
No noise to be heard
But the badgers sniffling.

Colette Langhorn (10)
St Thomas More RC Primary School, Kettering

Snow

The snow crunched under my frozen feet.
The fresh air under the snow,
Like frothy cream bubbling from a hot chocolate,
Or a newborn lamb's spotless coat.
A sprinkle of freezing snow trickled down my back,
Smoothly and gently it went.
The snow glistened, gleamed and glimmered.
A hedgehog snuggled in a corner.
A dazzling white carpet under my feet.
The snow is still as white as a feather.

Sheena Hamilton (9)
St Thomas More RC Primary School, Kettering

Snow

Soft, pure, white snow,
Gliding through the blackened sky
And silently forming a carpet of white,
While citizens slept unaware
Of the marvellous snow falling.

Deep was the bed of pure white snow
By the time the cockerel crowed
It was almost a metre thick,
So when the citizens emerged
It was at least three feet deep!

So when young children set out to play,
They marvelled at the sight!

A carpet of glistening and sparkling white snow,
Lying across gravel, grass and stone.
Children's cries of amusement and glee
Will flood the crisp, cool January air!

Joe Pelley (10)
St Thomas More RC Primary School, Kettering

Snow Poem

White snow tumbling in the street.
It's like a carpet of white powder.
The powdery snow sailing to the ground,
Silent snow, cold and crisp.
The snowflakes fall twizzling, twirling, dancing in the air.
Everyone is shivering.
Snowflakes slither on my neck and slide down my back.

Tom Androsiuk (10)
St Thomas More RC Primary School, Kettering

Snow

From the sky the snow falls,
Snow is soft and pure white,
It falls from the sky onto the towns,
Like sprinkled icing sugar through a sieve.

Snow falling from the midnight sky,
The moon glowing like a star,
Swirling, whirling the snow falls,
Dancing and prancing to the ground.

In the morning the children wake up,
All excited, waiting to play,
People building snowmen big and round,
Wishing and praying the snow stays around!

Hannah McNally (9)
St Thomas More RC Primary School, Kettering

My Snow Poem

On a cold winter's night when the snow falls down,
It's cold and crisp,
So icy and sharp like a knifepoint,
Silent, calm, spongy like a crumb,
A mountain of snow begins to fall onto the concrete ground.
The snowflakes fall on rooftops,
Like sugar being sprinkled on cereals.
Snow drifting down like sugar,
Sparkling, glistening in the air,
Cities are covered with a carpet of white.

Anaise Spriggs (10)
St Thomas More RC Primary School, Kettering

The Snow Is . . .

The snow is falling from the sky,
Everyone is looking up high.
On the floor is dazzling white,
I think I'm going to have a snowball fight.

The snow is spinning, whirling and swooping from the morning sky,
The snow is a white carpet catching my eye.
The snow is chilly and the air is misty.

The snow is silent, the snow is soft.
It looks like a cup of hot chocolate froth.
I cannot see any of the ground
And I can only hear one sound.

Sarah Lambe (10)
St Thomas More RC Primary School, Kettering

Snow

Snow is slippery along the frozen ground.
Snow is like shining crystal jewels.
Snow is like sifting icing sugar,
Softly falling snow touches the towns.
Children playing in the still snow,
Unaccustomed to the snow.
Seven inches high and really thick.
Soft and smooth, silent and still.

Emma-Louise Humphrey (10)
St Thomas More RC Primary School, Kettering

Snow

In the dark moonlit night,
Snow floats to the floor
Swiftly and silently,
Like icing sugar on a cake.

Mario Di Fazio
St Thomas More RC Primary School, Kettering

A Snow Poem

Twisting and twirling throughout the day and night,
When people come out, what a beautiful sight!
In the midnight air snow swaying
Sprinkling everywhere.
But the silent snow still goes on even though it's night,
Swirling and whirling
Glowing and glistening.
People gazing at the snow
Looks like a ballet in the theatre one says
Snow takes different shapes.
More like a swarm of white bees whirling through the air,
The other says.
It takes a thin layer of snow on rooftops, trees, cars and the ground.
Looks like icing sugar being sprinkled everywhere.
Snow becomes thicker and thicker.

Evie Hall (10)
St Thomas More RC Primary School, Kettering

Snow

I awoke one shivering, cold morning
To find that it was snowing.
I hurried out into the blazing mist of snow.
I set off to build a snowman.
I dashed into my house,
Slamming the door
Grabbing my hat, scarf
And a carrot from the nose.
Coal for the eyes, mouth and buttons,
A twig from the ground for the arms.
At last it was finished!
'Mum! Dad!' I cried. 'Come see!'

Rosie Dougherty (9)
St Thomas More RC Primary School, Kettering

Weather

Howling hurricanes hammer houses
Whistling winds whoosh through woods
Terrible tornadoes terrorise towns
Smashing storms steal sun

Worrying weather wrecks warehouse walls
Raindrops rush, rattling down the road
Fierce floods frighten forest folk
Lashing lightning lights late night sky.

Forest fires fight firemen
Drought dries Denmark
Washing definitely drying
Windy weather wails at windows.

Paul Milligan (11)
St Thomas More RC Primary School, Kettering

Snow Poem

As I woke up this morning I heard a noise,
But then I heard the boys.
I looked out the window to find that it was snowing.
All the houses covered with the dazzling magic.
As the snow was twirling through,
And the snow was falling,
All the boys were having fun.
But the snow still came down, down and down.
The street was a magical sheet of snow.

Callum Kennedy (10)
St Thomas More RC Primary School, Kettering

Snow Haiku

Snow, the sparkling snow,
Snow sneaking silently, like
A fox in the night.

Heidi Judge (9)
St Thomas More RC Primary School, Kettering

A Snow Poem

Pitter-pattering on the ground,
Snow dazzling on my paper round.
That's all you can hear, the only sound.
Flying, then lying on the roof,
Glistening sparkles in the night.
What a beautiful sight.

Dazzling snow was flying.
It twirled and whirled and then lay lying.
The snow was twinkling in the sky,
Up above and oh so high.

Rebecca Johnson (10)
St Thomas More RC Primary School, Kettering

Snow

I woke up one day
In my dark bedroom.
I crept downstairs
Into the silent kitchen.
I peeped out of the misty window.
There was snow falling down from the white sky.
The snow that fell in the silent night.

James Henderson (10)
St Thomas More RC Primary School, Kettering

'Woof!' Said The Cat

'Woof!' said the cat.
'Squeak!' said the dog.
'Oink!' said the mosquito.
'Cluck!' said the hog.

'Miaow!' said the pig.
'Tweet!' said the frog.
'Moo!' said the fox
That ran through the fog.

'Quack!' said the snake.
'Hee-haw!' said the sow.
'Cheep-cheep!' said the cockerel.
'Baa!' said the cow.

James Percival (11)
St Thomas More RC Primary School, Kettering

Snow Poem

Snow is falling all around
Softly, softly to the ground.
Delicate snowflakes sifting down
Floating gently like a cloud.

When I woke up this morning
I was amazed at the sight!
The trees were covered with white fleece
And the ground was a carpet of white.

Rosie Elmore (9)
St Thomas More RC Primary School, Kettering

I Don't Know Why

The wet, watery wind
blows away rubber rubbish from bins.
The moaning, howling hurricane
hustling, bustling like a cane.
Freezing people's cold feet
while eating their lovely treats.
People sit on the park seat
while a fleet of bees buzz by
I think I don't know why!

George Martin (10)
St Thomas More RC Primary School, Kettering

I, The Wind

I blow the clothes upon the line
They swish and turn and jump about
I blow upon the chimney tops
Moaning, mooing and puffing.
The trees start to dance as I give them a gust.
Sends chills down children's spines.
All wrapped up from head to toe
To go to the park away they go.

Ashleigh Earley (11)
St Thomas More RC Primary School, Kettering